From Digital Divide to Digital Opportunity

Appu Kuttan and Laurence Peters

ScarecrowEducation
Lanham, Maryland • Toronto • Oxford
2003

A SCARECROWEDUCATION BOOK

Published in the United States of America
by ScarecrowEducation
An imprint of The Rowman & Littlefield Publishing Group, Inc.
4501 Forbes Boulevard, Suite 200, Lanham, Maryland 20706
www.scarecroweducation.com

PO Box 317
Oxford
OX2 9RU, UK

British Library Cataloguing in Publication Information Available

Library of Congress Cataloging-in-Publication Data

Kuttan, Appu, 1941–
    From digital divide to digital opportunity / Appu Kuttan, Laurence Peters.
        p. cm.
    Includes bibliographical references and index.
    ISBN 0-8108-4491-5 (alk. paper)—ISBN 0-8108-4492-3 (pbk. : alk. paper)
        1. Digital divide—United States. 2. Digital divide. 3. Information technology—Social
    aspects—United States. I. Peters, Laurence, 1952– II. Title.

HN90.156 K888 2003
303.48'33—dc21

2002030296

♾️™ The paper used in this publication meets the minimum requirements of American
National Standard for Information Sciences—Permanence of Paper for Printed Library
Materials, ANSI/NISO Z39.48-1992.
Manufactured in the United States of America.

Contents

Preface

A widening disparity between information/technology haves and have-nots (the "digital divide") threatens the prosperity of individuals, businesses, and communities around the world. However, problems bring opportunities, and enormous opportunities abound for political, business, and community leaders with the vision to take their communities/countries from digital divide via digital opportunity to higher levels of prosperity.

This book is a result of our dynamic real-life experience with digital divide problems, programs, and solutions both in the United States and in other countries. Anyone interested in learning about the digital divide—students, teachers, administrators, community members, political leaders, government leaders, and community leaders—should read this book to take advantage of our many years of experience in policymaking, planning, and implementing holistic digital divide bridging programs, both in the nonprofit and government sectors. We provide practical suggestions for planning and implementing cost-effective digital opportunity programs that bridge the digital divide.

The world will change more in the next thirty years than in all of the twentieth century. Information technology (IT) will be the main driving force for that change. Hence, it is imperative that individuals as well as communities and nations approach the future strategically.

Our interest in the digital divide goes back to 1993 when we identified the "growing gap between information technology haves and have-nots" as a serious problem in the emerging Information Age. After discussions with President Bill Clinton, Vice President Al Gore, and many other national leaders (including Intel founder Gordon Moore), we set up the nonprofit CyberLearning (www.cyberlearning.org) with the goal of training a million disadvantaged students in information technology skills.

One of the first national projects we carried out in 1995 involved taking a fifty-foot van equipped with Internet-accessible computers to the poor inner cities and rural areas in the United States, and demonstrating to teachers, students, school administrators, and parents how to use the Internet as a learning tool. For the next few years, we offered many classroom programs in IT topics to disadvantaged students and adults.

Despite these important efforts to place the digital divide issues on the national agenda, by the end of the decade, we realized that many digital divide programs were failing because they offered only piecemeal solutions. Many programs simply involved putting wires and boxes into classrooms, or providing recycled computers to disadvantaged schools. It became clear to us that without properly trained teachers, adequate Internet access, or good content/courseware, these isolated approaches were neither effective nor sustainable.

The digital divide is a systemic problem, requiring a holistic total solution to training students in IT; this is why we developed the Cyber-Learning concept. This concept, also known as TTCM, integrates the four key components of a training program: trained Teachers/training, adequate Technology (hardware, software, access), engaging Courseware and content, and proper Motivation to help students achieve their learning goals cost effectively.

We recognized that, in order to implement a holistic IT training program, we needed to provide teacher training, courseware access, and mentors who could nurture students through the often new and challenging process of classroom as well as online learning. In 1999, we started offering high-quality online Web-based courses for a low fee to the teachers and students of disadvantaged schools, colleges, and nonprofit organizations. Since then, we have added online courses in management and test-prep (SAT, etc.) skills. We developed these online approaches to be used in conjunction with formal academic or community programs that serve great numbers of individuals in school or who have either dropped out of formal schooling or who find it too expensive or too difficult to fit training into their work schedules.

Currently, CyberLearning offers over a thousand online Web-based interactive courses from high-quality course providers, including Harvard Business School Publishing, Element K, Mindleaders, and Barrons Education to disadvantaged schools, colleges, and nonprofits for a very low monthly fee, often less than the cost of a McDonald's meal! To bridge the national digital divide, we also offer matching grants to organizations to train teachers as well as to purchase the missing parts of hardware, software, and Internet access, to enable them to implement holistic solutions. To bridge the global digital divide, we have started CyberLearning programs in many countries, including India, Egypt, and Jordan. We hope to provide cost-effective, high-quality CyberLearning courses and programs to entire school districts, college networks, communities, counties, cities, states, and countries in the next few years, thus helping to bridge both the U.S. national and global digital divide.

Out of the many examples of the successful digital divide bridging programs in this book, one example stands out. Singapore, a Third World country just a few years ago, has become a developed country by providing educational and digital opportunities to its entire population. The Singapore program primarily focused on improving education at all levels, wiring all schools to the Internet, and providing substantial professional development for their teachers. Singapore offers a model for everyone to follow. Singapore's high living standard was not achieved by accident but rather through planned strategic investments.

If visionary leaders make the right strategic decisions, disadvantaged communities and nations have a unique historic opportunity to leapfrog into a higher standard of living in a few years rather than go through the evolutionary period of decades. An important message to be taken from this book is that today's leaders must study the lessons of countries like Singapore and communities around the globe that have decided to become digital communities if they want to become full participants in the twenty-first-century global knowledge economy. The recent Hudson Institute study, indicating that 85 percent of the careers with the highest job growth today require technology skills, clearly supports the view that providing digital opportunities for an entire community will enhance the prosperity of that community.

Research for this book has convinced us that the digital divide is a constantly evolving theme, and it needs serious attention from all parties concerned, especially political leaders. The tragic September 11th events have reinforced our belief that education and the Internet can provide better opportunities for the disadvantaged globally, and thus lead to better economic conditions and less terrorism.

We are grateful to the many organizations and individuals who have assisted us directly and indirectly with this book. For the development of this book itself, we feel a deep sense of gratitude to:

- Our spouses, Claudia Kuttan and Michele Peters
- Our children, Roger and Maya Kuttan; Noah, Jonathan, and Emma Peters
- Our research assistants, Dan Larkin, India Owen, and Will Nesbitt
- The happy memories of our parents

This book includes one of the largest reference sources for the digital divide. We hope that this book will continue to evolve with both CyberLearning and the digital divide. We would appreciate your input (send to: digitaldivide@cyberlearning.org) for enhancing this book with more ideas, examples of successful programs, facts, and so forth. Those of you interested in becoming a CyberLearning partner, and thus becoming eligible for matching grants for bridging the digital divide, may visit www.cyberlearning.org and click on the "partners" link.

We sincerely hope that this book will inspire you to do your part in providing digital opportunities to your family, friends, and community members, and thus make this global village a better place for all humanity in this twenty-first-century Information Age.

CHAPTER 1

Defining the Digital Divide

The Internet is a hall of mirrors. In its multiple images, its uses reflect the inequalities and injustices of the societies into which it is inserted. Thus, information technologies are not positive or negative in themselves; but neither are they neutral. They take the form and direction of the societies in which they are introduced, and at the same time they help further shape the relations and modes of interaction in these societies.

—Ricardo Gomez[1]

Summary:

Putting the digital divide in context to today's political and economic environment, this chapter frames the policy debate surrounding the digital divide by:

- Tracing the evolution of the digital divide,
- Objectively presenting the opposing opinions on the Internet's actual value, and
- Analyzing the Internet through the prism of universal service as opposed to universal access.

With this as background, the status of the digital divide in the United States in 2002 is explored. Special focus is given to the emerging "broadband divide," in addition to the digital divide's impact on low-income groups, minorities, seniors, individuals with disabilities, rural communities, and women.

Eighth-graders in a private, suburban school take their seats in the school's computer lab. There is no rushing or jockeying for seats; the lab has more than enough computers. Without prompting from the instructor, the students expertly navigate through the Internet, confidently mining for information. After all, most of them have computers of their own at home to practice on. A few miles down the road, yet a world away, eighth-graders at a public school sign in for their turn at one of the school's three computers. The line is long but moves steadily because the school enforces a fifteen-minute time limit. It is almost ironic that the students' fifteen minutes can feel like an eternity as the old computers wheeze and stall through the Internet. But the students can always sign up for another fifteen minutes tomorrow.

Welcome to the digital divide.

WHAT IS THE DIGITAL DIVIDE?

"Digital divide" has become a popular term recently. It has become a favorite phrase for academics and pundits, educators and politicians. Unfortunately, it has been misused and overused so often that it has become just another amorphous catchphrase that has clouded the real and pressing problem that it represents.

So, what is the digital divide? Opinions vary on the technological nature of the digital divide (see figure 1.1) and how it divides society (see figure 1.2).

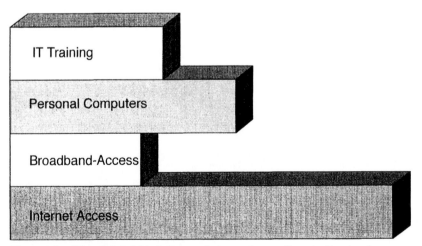

Figure 1.1. *"The digital divide is the gap between those with and without . . ."*

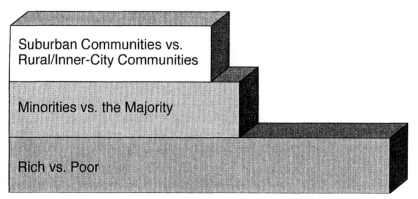

Figure 1.2.   *"The digital divide is a gap between . . ."*

In the broadest sense, the digital divide is the gap between those people and communities who have access to information technology (personal computers, the Internet, skills, etc.) and those who do not.[2] In other words, it is the disparity between the technology "haves" and the "have-nots."

Some, notably President George W. Bush, argue that use of "digital divide" is tantamount to class warfare; he sees the problems as an "achievement gap."[3] His platform stresses "digital opportunity"—expanding and ensuring the growth of a technology-dependent economy by strengthening the existing systems that built it.[4] Further, President Bush's chairman of the Federal Communications Commission, Michael Powell, has called the term digital divide "dangerous" because "it suggests that the minute a new and innovative technology comes to market there is a divide unless it's equitably distributed among every part of society . . . and if companies think they can't produce a new product unless they can produce it cheap enough for all, it could deter them from innovating and offering new goods."[5]

Carly Fiorina, CEO of Hewlett Packard, suggests the term e-inclusion to emphasize the importance of improving science and math education and providing universal Internet access.[6] Others stress the terms digital inclusion, digital renaissance, or info-exclusion.[7] The controversy on the wording of "digital divide" offers an insight into the larger debate on how to solve the real problem of the divide, as will be discussed later in this book.

Semantics aside, for the purposes of this book, the term digital divide—defined as the gaps in technology, access to technology (specifically the Internet), education, and technology training between and within specific populations—will be used.

BRIEF OUTLINE OF THE EVOLUTION OF THE DIGITAL DIVIDE

In the United States, the term digital divide was given wide currency in the mid-1990s. At that time, the nation's political leaders realized that although the country enjoyed unprecedented economic growth (in large part stimulated by the growth of technology), many groups had been left behind by the economic boom. Many contrasted the economic success of those with access to technology with the economic stagnation of those lacking that access. Furthermore, it was not a purely economic issue. Technology access had increasingly enmeshed itself with educational, social, and political opportunities.[8] A correlation was drawn: those with better access to technology are better prepared to succeed and prosper in the new technology-driven economy and society—the Information Age.

In public policy terms, this meant that those without access to technology would fall behind those with access, forming an "information underclass"[9] and thus separating society with a widening economic and social gap—a digital divide. At the heart of the issue is the ability (or inability) of people to participate fully in the new Information Age that ensures "equality of opportunity in social, educational, political, and economic systems."[10]

Realizing the potential harm of the growing digital divide, the U.S. Department of Commerce commissioned a series of groundbreaking reports. The "Falling through the Net" reports vividly described the growing gap between the types of computer access available in educated, high-income, mostly urban, homes, as opposed to less-educated, poorer households. Some of the sobering facts presented in the reports included:

- Urban households earning incomes over $75,000 are over twenty times more likely to have home Internet access than rural households at the lowest income levels.
- While a significant majority of Americans (58.9 percent) making over $75,000 frequent the Internet from any location, many fewer persons (16.0 percent) at the lower end of the pay scale ($5,000–$10,000) use the Internet.
- Those earning under $20,000 and using the Internet outside the home are twice as likely (2.12 times) to get access through a public library or community center than those earning more than $20,000.[11]

The most jarring fact was that from 1997 to 1998, the digital divide for home Internet access between those at the highest and lowest income levels widened by 29 percent.[12]

With the digital divide now entrenched in public policy debate, President Bill Clinton said in his 2000 State of the Union Address, "Opportunity for all requires something else today—having access to a computer and knowing how to use it. That means we must close the digital divide between those who've got the tools and those who don't. Connecting classrooms and libraries to the Internet is crucial, but it's just a start."[13] The digital divide had grown into a top policy matter. President Clinton stressed the urgency of the problem: "This is a national crusade. We have got to [close the digital divide], and do it quickly." [14]

Echoing Clinton's sentiments, Vice President Gore made closing the digital divide an integral part of his 2000 presidential campaign. Gore proclaimed that, as president, he would "make sure every American has the ABCs of the Internet: access, basic skills, and high-quality content"[15] and would "make Internet access as common as the telephone."[16] For his part, candidate George W. Bush stated that the "real divide is in educational achievement, not just digital access."[17]

Like the rapid advancement of the technology that spawned it, the digital divide evolved swiftly from theory to statistical fact to the center of policy debate. Before the current state of the digital divide can be discussed, the terms of the digital divide debate need closer examination.

TERMS OF THE DIGITAL DIVIDE DEBATE IN THE UNITED STATES

The digital divide in the United States is usually measured in terms of personal computer ownership and Internet access. These rates are compared between major demographic categories (race, income, age, disability, location [rural/urban], education, and gender) and combinations of the categories (for example, low-income Hispanics). Table 1.1 illustrates how these comparisons are made. As an example, this table breaks down the major demographics (with the exception of disability) for the five states with the lowest percentage of household computer ownership: Arkansas, Louisiana, Mississippi, Oklahoma, and West Virginia.[18]

Although this table could be interpreted to "prove" the digital divide (lower incomes and lower educational levels mean less computer ownership and Internet access), that is not its purpose. Rather, its intention

Table 1.1. Household Computer Ownership

	% of households owning a computer	% of households w/ Internet access	% of Internet connectivity for households w/ computers	Average income ($)	% living in poverty	% w/ college education	% of minorities	% of women	People per sq. mile
AR	38.5	14.8	48.97	28,389	16.4	10.5	19.3	51.6	49
LA	42	18.6	57.48	33,218	18.2	12	36.4	51.8	100.4
MS	38.7	13.6	51.68	30,628	16.8	11	38.3	52	59
OK	42.1	21	54.13	33,311	13.5	14	20.4	51.1	48.9
WV	43	17.5	61.35	28,420	16.7	10	4.2	53.2	75
US	**51**	**26.2**	**61.8**	**39,657**	**12.6**	**16**	**28.1**	**51.1**	**77.1**

is to demonstrate who the digital divide debate is focused on (the major demographic categories) and how the digital divide is measured (Internet access, computer ownership). A detailed discussion of the major demographics follows later in this chapter.

The policy debate on the digital divide has its roots in the notions of universal service and universal access, long a part of telecommunications in the United States. As its name implies, the goal of universal service is to provide affordable telephone service to all Americans. The mechanism to accomplish this takes the form of cross-subsidies: urban phone users subsidize rural phone users; businesses subsidize residential users; and long-distance fees subsidize local exchanges.

The goal of universal access, often viewed as the precursor to universal service, is to provide telephone service within a "reasonable distance" for everyone: that is, public payphones.[19] Universal access policies emphasize increased access to telecommunication at a community-wide and not a personal level. [20]

The reasoning behind universal service policies is threefold. First, universal service is seen as a necessity for American democracy: citizens "cannot effectively participate in the democratic process if they do not have equal and unrestricted access to the main methods of communication."[21] Second, universal service is needed to ensure "equal opportunity," both socially and economically, for all.[22] Third, universal service promotes self-advancement; for example, basic telecommunication service is "necessary to hold a good job and seek out better opportunities."[23]

As policy, universal service was broadened to include Internet access in 1996. The Schools and Libraries Universal Service Fund, popularly known as the E-Rate, was created as part of the Telecommunications Act of 1996 to ensure that all eligible schools and libraries in the United States have affordable access "to modern telecommunications and information services," meaning, in practical terms, the Internet.[24] The E-Rate budget is capped at $2.25 billion annually[25] with funding provided by the telecommunications industry (generated, in turn, by cross-subsidies). E-Rate provides schools and libraries with discounts according to their level of economic disadvantage (based on the percentage of students eligible for the national school lunch program) and their location (rural or urban).[26] E-Rate funds can only be used to pay for a school or library's internal connections, telecommunications services, and Internet access. The theory is that the money the schools and libraries save on their telecommunications infrastructure can pay for the computers, software, and teacher/librarian training necessary to make the Internet access worthwhile and thus accomplish the goal of helping to bridge the digital divide.

The fact that E-Rate was the first extension of universal service beyond common carriage[27] was and is the source of much debate. The crux of the E-Rate debate mirrors that at the core of the digital divide debate: Is this actually a crisis that warrants dramatic action, or is it the latest policy fad that distracts attention away from more urgent needs?

Digital Divide: Crisis or Hype?

Central in the policy debate is the question of the actual importance of the digital divide. Like many policy controversies, this core question has polarized the players in the debate into two camps: those who feel the digital divide is a legitimate crisis and those who think the problem has been overblown by media-fueled hype.

The Digital Divide: Crisis?

Armed with such startling statistics as 35 percent of those in the lower socioeconomic strata have access to the Internet, as opposed to 85 percent in the higher classes[28] and that any combination of two major demographic categories (listed above) lowers Internet access rates by 200 to 300 percent,[29] some argue that the digital divide is a crisis of monumental proportions.

Bridging the digital divide is often referred to in terms of an epic undertaking. Putting the digital divide on par with the massive effort to rebuild Europe after World War II, U.S. Congressman John Larson declared that America needs a "technological Marshall Plan" to overcome the digital divide and "if we don't close the gap, the nation will be in peril."[30] This echoes the tone of President Clinton's "national call to action on closing the digital divide"[31] — that the digital divide warrants a colossal, communal effort like the New Deal or the War on Poverty. In the same vein, the digital divide has been called "one of the most important civil rights issues facing our modern Information society." [32] Harkening back to the imagery of the Civil Rights struggles of the 1960s, the digital divide threatens to create "cyberghettoes"[33] where those without equal access to technology "will be further segregated into the periphery of public life."[34]

To this end, the "crisis mentality" of the digital divide has spurred Representative Larson and other like-minded members of the U.S. Congress to push for the Home Internet Access Program (HIAP) and the Technology Opportunity Program (TOP). HIAP would allocate $50 million for targeted investments to bring low-income and at-risk groups online; TOP would provide $45 million in matching funds for state, local, and tribal governments to extend information technologies in underserved communities.[35] It was viewed that HIAP and TOP would be beachheads in the vast battle to close the digital divide.

The Digital Divide: Hype?

On the other end of the policy-debate spectrum are those who feel that the digital divide has been purposely exaggerated and is far from a crisis. After all, they say, most people only use computers and the Internet for entertainment and convenience and those without this technology are "not facing an imperiled future."[36] Many scoff at the idea of the digital divide as a crisis: "World hunger, wars, AIDS, and environmental decay are crises. When the Internet can solve these problems, [then] maybe everyone needs to have a computer."[37]

Also, the digital divide is just the latest in a long history of economic gaps. In the words of Mark Lloyd, executive director of the Civil Rights Forum on Communications Policy, "We had the agricultural divide when our economy was based on agriculture. We had the industrial divide when our economy was based on . . . industry. . . . [Now, with a high-tech based economy,] it's not a surprise that we have a digital divide."[38] Along these same lines (even though he personally has donated millions of dollars to bridge the digital divide), Microsoft Chairman Bill Gates questioned the very idea of the digital divide when he said, "most of the world doesn't have cars, but we don't talk about the auto divide."[39] Putting a snide spin on Gates' sentiment, FCC Chairman Michael Powell said of the digital divide: "I think there's a Mercedes divide. . . . I'd like to have one, but can't afford one."[40]

Many in this camp also feel that the time is past when the digital divide could possibly have been called a crisis. They argue that four or five years ago, when a home computer cost nearly $2,000 and Internet access was steeply priced on a per hour basis, there existed a real digital divide. But now, they claim, the wide availability of much more affordable technology has made debating the digital divide as pointless as fretting about the Y2K computer bug. As writer Adam Clayton

Powell III commented, "With dirt-cheap Internet access and computers approaching the cost of television sets, assertions of a 'digital divide' . . . are as correct as . . . pinning last week's Dow at 1,000."[41]

The naysayers often point to an April 2000 report by Forrester Research to buttress their position. The conclusion of the research in the Forrester report is that although the digital divide has garnered a lot of media coverage by suggesting that while minorities lag behind online, not all minorities are on the wrong side of the divide. For example, Internet penetration among Asian Americans is higher than for Whites. Furthermore, once online, the digital divide virtually disappears because, regardless of ethnicity, all consumers use the Internet for the same things—e-mail, shopping, and entertainment.[42]

Internet Access: Necessity or Luxury?

This leads to another facet of the digital divide debate: whether the Internet is actually a necessity of modern life, or merely a convenience, or even a luxury.

The Internet: Necessity?

Those who believe it is a necessity draw the ready parallel between telephone access and Internet access. In their eyes, the Internet is to communication in the twenty-first century what the telephone was in the twentieth. The Internet inherits the telephone's ideal of universal service: because it is so vital for communication, every single person has the right to have access to it. If we cannot expect a person without a telephone to have the same advantages and opportunities as the vast majority who do, then we cannot expect the same advantages and opportunities are available to a person without Internet access.

The parallel is also drawn between Internet access and literacy. Many believe that the modern definition of literacy must be expanded to include information literacy. Information literacy is the ability to "access, evaluate, organize, and use information from a variety of sources."[43] In essence, information literacy is the ability to take raw information and transform it into useful knowledge.[44] Those who are information illiterate are just as economically, socially, and culturally handcuffed as someone who cannot read or write. One report estimates that, due to a lack of knowledge of or access to the Internet, a whole generation of Americans—50 million people—is in danger of becoming "functionally illiterate" because they lack information literacy.[45] This does not bode well for the future. The U.S. Department of Labor considers information literacy as "one of the five essential competencies necessary for solid job performance."[46]

The most powerful argument on why Internet access is a necessity is that because the Internet has become so entwined and integral in today's society, society has been transformed by it. As President Clinton's Chief of Staff John Podesta put it: "Information and communication technologies have altered the way we play, work and do business. . . . [Information technology has caused] one of the most fundamental transformations in our country's history."[47] Therefore, it is absolutely essential to have access to such an influential shaper of society like the Internet. The impact of the Internet does not go understated: A widely cited report calls the Internet the "most important technological development of our generation" that could, over time, "equal the influence of the printing press."[48] In a functioning democracy, something that powerful must be accessible.

There is a wealth of examples of how the Internet has transformed society. For instance, in 1998 the U.S. Postal Service delivered *only* 101 billion pieces of paper mail, while Americans sent an estimated 4 trillion e-mails in that same year.[49] E-mail has become a fundamental means of communication, with 42 percent of Americans using it every day.[50] Furthermore, approximately half of the traffic on the national telephone network is Internet traffic.[51]

Another prime example is that in 2000, approximately 35.4 million Americans filed their federal income taxes online with more than 40 million projected to do so in 2001.[52] Moreover, the 2.5 million businesses that filed their federal taxes online in 1999 accounted for 84 percent of all business tax revenue.[53]

A further example of how the Internet is transforming society is in health care. More than 10 percent of all the information on the Internet is health-related[54] and 45 percent of people online search for health information on the Internet.[55] A specific illustration of how the Internet has changed health care is California's Long Beach Community Medical Center, which offers area residents Internet links to HMOs affiliated with the hospital, replacing the HMOs' ponderously long physicians rosters with a sophisticated doctor-referral program.[56] Patients at Long Beach Community Medical Center can also enroll in an HMO and register for a hospital visit, all online.[57]

Just as the Internet transformed society, it revolutionized business. Sixty-seven percent of workers believe the Internet is "essential" for the work they do.[58] On a much broader scale, in recent years, information technology industries have been responsible for more than one-fourth of real economic growth in the United States.[59] In 1999, the Internet directly supported 1.2 million jobs.[60] That number skyrocketed to 3.088 million in 2000.[61] Moreover, the Internet added $135 billion to the economy in 1999[62] and $406.6 billion in 2000.[63] And while these figures might appear moot in light of the recent well-publicized bust of many "dot.com" companies, it must be realized that dot.coms only account for 9.6 percent of the entire Internet industry.[64] To date, the Internet still supports 60,000 more jobs than the insurance industry and close to double the number of jobs of the real estate industry.[65] Therefore, to deny people access to such a huge segment of the economy as the Internet is to shut the door of economic advancement and prosperity in their faces.

The Internet: Luxury?

Opposing this view are those who see the value of the Internet as overrated at best. Yes, they concede, with the Internet you can file your taxes, schedule a doctor's appointment, or any other worthwhile endeavor. But is that what the Internet is really used for? No, they assert, apparently it is used more as a medium for smut. Research indicates that of all the terms searched for online, 0.3289 percent (or approximately 1 of every 300 terms) are "sex."[66] People search online for "sex" more often than the terms "games," "music," "travel," "jokes," "cars," "jobs," "weather," and "health" *combined*.[67] Plus, "porn" (with its variants "porno" and "pornography") is the fourth most popular Internet search term.[68] And if that is not enough, the terms "nude," "xxx," "playboy," and "erotica" are all among the top twenty searched-for words on the Internet.[69] In light of this, they argue, who can claim the Internet is a necessity? Dirty old men?

Beyond this, those who view the importance of access to the Internet as overemphasized tend to focus their arguments on the role of the Internet and education. After all, students (specifically children) are often cited as those who will benefit the greatest from the Internet. Opponents of the significance of students' access to the Internet say that it confuses educational priorities. The debate on Internet access draws attention away from the real issues of education: learning reading, writing, and arithmetic in safe schools where the roofs do not leak and that are staffed by well-trained teachers.

Critics point to the generally mediocre performance of American students in the fundamentals and ask what good is the Internet to students if they have troubles with basic reading and math? Some express the opinion that America's failing education system is the real digital divide. Is it unreasonable to assume that if students cannot find their home state on a map, they could gain anything from a home page on the Internet? In other words, "if children cannot read, write, or master basic arithmetic, all the wonders of the Internet are beyond their reach, even if a computer is within it." [70]

As Tom Lipscomb, president of the Center of the Digital Future said, "[Society] better worry about the fact that failure of basic education does not go well with the computer-based, highly unforgiving environment of the Internet . . . if you can't spell you can't URL."[71] Likewise, MIT professor David Gelernter says that claiming it is necessary for students to have access to the Internet is like demanding "every child must have the fanciest scuba gear on the market—but [if] these kids don't know how to swim . . . fitting them out with scuba gear isn't just useless, it's irresponsible; they'll drown."[72]

To critics, focusing on the Internet ignores the real problems in education. Christopher Foreman, a senior fellow at the Brookings Institution, derides the value of Internet technology in education: "We have existing technology called 'books' that are currently in existing neighborhood centers called 'libraries.' We already have a problem getting young people to use this existing technology. It makes me nervous that people will focus on the digital divide without paying attention to the old-fashioned paper divide."[73] Doubt is also cast upon the real value of the Internet to a student's education. Will students use the Internet to do research? Yes . . . sometimes. But in reality, they will spend most of their time exchanging instant messages with friends, playing games, chatting in chat rooms, and downloading music. How do these activities improve a student's education?

Who Is Not "Wired" and Why?

On the surface, the most recent reports on Internet access in the United States would indicate that the digital divide is shrinking. As of January 2001, 60 percent of the American population has access to the Internet, with a total of 162 million Americans using the Internet from school, home, or work.[74] But before any champagne is popped, some facts behind these figures must be revealed. This report measured the entire U.S. population—which means it counted everyone above the age of two years old, including, obviously, all the under-eighteen students who have access in their schools.[75] Furthermore, "access" means you could get online; so, for example, all 600 students of a school with four Internet-connected computers are considered to have access.

Looking at the adult population, the picture becomes less rosy. Half of the adults in the United States do not have Internet access.[76] This "unwired" population can be broken down into four major groups: nonusers due to usability issues, nonusers due to lack of education, nonusers due to governmental/regulatory barriers, and voluntary nonusers. For our purposes, only the first three groups of nonusers will be discussed.

Usability

Of the "unwired," 36 percent say that the Internet is confusing and difficult.[77] For these people, the digital divide is really a usability problem that cannot be bridged unless computers and the Internet are made significantly easier to use. Evidence of usability problems can be found in a study that tracked Internet users' searching techniques. Instead of entering a URL in the address field of their Web browsers, millions of Internet users type the name of the site they want into the search field of a search engine.[78] For example, to go to the website for Yahoo!, many people would type in "www.yahoo.com" into their search engine, not realizing that it is easier and more efficient to enter the address directly into the browser. This is significant because it reveals a "conceptual misunderstanding"[79] of the Internet and that the Internet is "still a technical hurdle many people have not yet cleared."[80] And these are people who have some comfort level and experience with the Internet. Now imagine how befuddling the Internet must appear for a nonuser.

Lack of Education

From a variety of studies, it is clear that a person's educational level is a major factor in determining if they are "wired" or not.

- A University of Massachusetts study found that as education increased so does the likelihood of owning a computer: 60 percent of those with college degrees own a computer while 70 percent of those with a high school education or less do not own a computer.[81]

- A study by Stanford University concluded that the major factor facilitating Internet access is education: those with a college degree are 49 percent more likely to have and use Internet access than those without a college degree.[82]
- A study by UCLA determined that the higher the educational level a person has, the more likely they are to use the Internet: 86.3 percent of those with either an undergraduate degree or advanced degree use the Internet.[83]
- The Pew Internet Project reports that 82 percent of those with a college degree and 71 percent of those with some college education have Internet access, compared to 37 percent of those with a high school education or less.[84]

Government/Regulatory Barriers

The third and final "unwired" group is perhaps the most crucial. These are the people who are hindered in getting broadband Internet access due to government and regulatory barriers. Their plight is important because broadband access is being trumpeted as the "great leap forward" in the Internet. And this group is part of the elite "early adopters" that will be critical to the eventual wide-acceptance of broadband technologies. Yet to many in this group who want broadband access and are willing to pay the premium to get it, access is difficult if not impossible to get.

This can be seen by the fact that government regulations on data transmission have impeded the deployment of the high-speed Internet backbone.[85] This governmental intrusion has resulted in some areas of the nation having no access to high-speed Internet connections.[86] Due to shortsighted government-imposed restrictions on data transmission, not enough Internet backbone hubs are being built outside of major business and population centers.[87] Without access to backbone hubs, users are forced to connect to the Internet with slower networks that cannot handle the bandwidth-heavy applications that are now common in e-commerce, telemedicine, and distance learning.[88] While some can access the Internet through advanced networks that deliver broadband applications at lightning speed, others must access the Internet "through the digital equivalent of a dirt road."[89]

Although this problem affects the entire nation, twelve states are suffering the most from the governmental regulations: Alabama, Arkansas,

Idaho, Iowa, Maine, Montana, New Hampshire, North Dakota, Oklahoma, South Dakota, West Virginia, and Wyoming.[90] For example, Arkansas currently has two hubs and New Hampshire has three.[91] If the government regulations on data transmission were lifted, it is predicted that these states would have 28 and 42 hubs, respectively.[92]

Where broadband is available, it is often local, state, or federal telecommunications regulations that are limiting access to individual users. For example, federal regulations forbid deploying data networks across random geographic lines while local zoning ordinances are often muddled and archaic and thus interfere with new services. In addition, many municipalities have "open access laws" that require the companies that build the broadband network to sell parts of their network at below cost. Cities like Portland, Oregon, have passed open access laws only to see their broadband expansion stall as the city and the service provider argue in court.[93] Who ultimately suffers from this regulatory wrangling? Those who simply want faster access to the Internet.

ASPECTS OF ACCESS

No matter one's viewpoint on the causes, effects, or even the existence of the digital divide, most agree the problem can be distilled down to an issue of access. While it is true to say the digital divide is about the gaps in access to the Internet, it also about access to broadband connections, access to computers and Internet devices, access to usable Internet content, and access to employment opportunities generated by the Internet. Each of these aspects of access deserves a closer examination.

Access to Broadband Connections

Access to telecommunication connections has evolved from an issue of who has a connection to the Internet to who has high-speed, or broadband, connections. Cable modems, DSL, and ADSL offer connections to the Internet at speeds hundreds of times faster than the typical dial-up connection. As Internet content becomes more bandwidth-intensive with the reliance on sound, video, and rich graphical images, broadband connections are crucial to many data-intensive applications like distance education and telemedicine. With the advent of these technologies, a new rift is spreading within the digital divide between those with the blazingly quick, always-on broadband connections, and those still mired down with the plodding "old" dial-up connections.

At first glance, it might appear that the broadband issue is resolving itself. For example, since 1999, DSL service has increased 157 percent and high-speed cable access has increased 59 percent.[94] However, in terms of actual users, only 10.7 percent of online households have broadband Internet access, which translates to only 4.4 percent of all U.S. households.[95] Although more people are using broadband services, the Federal Communications Commissions states that five groups are "particularly vulnerable" to not having broadband access: rural, inner-city, and minority citizens; tribal areas; and consumers in U.S. territories.[96]

Broadband service is now available in zip codes representing 91 percent of America's population,[97] yet that "availability is concentrated in affluent urban and suburban areas, which some experts say underscores a developing 'digital divide' along lines of income and race."[98] Those areas with little or no high-speed access tend to be communities with higher concentrations of minorities and lower-income residents, such as inner-city areas.[99] The FCC reports that there is at least one broadband user in 90 percent of the zip codes serving affluent communities, while there is at least one broadband subscriber in only 42 percent of the zip codes serving low-income communities.[100]

Other telling statistics on income and broadband access include:

- America's wealthiest households use broadband connections 180 percent more than the nation's poorest households.[101]
- Forty percent of broadband users have an annual household income of $75,000 or more, compared to just 20 percent of dial-up users.[102]
- The average median household income is approximately 28 percent higher in the local areas where both DSL and cable modem service are available ($35,633) than the local areas where neither broadband service is available ($27,822).[103]
- Poverty rates are considerably lower in local areas where both DSL and cable modem service are available (10.24 percent) compared to local areas where neither broadband service is available (14.5 percent).[104]
- The average median home value is over 63 percent higher in local areas where both DSL and cable modem service are available ($124,265) than where neither broadband service is available ($76,015).[105]

In addition, educational level appears to be a factor: 27 percent of residents aged twenty-five and over have a college or advanced degree in areas where both DSL and cable modem service are available, compared to 19 percent in areas where neither service is available.[106]

Rural communities also are often on the wrong side of the broadband digital divide. Broadband subscribers are present in 96 percent of the most densely populated zip codes yet in only 40 percent of zip codes with the lowest population densities.[107] Furthermore:

- While cities have a 12.2 percent broadband connection rate (among households with Internet access), rural areas have only a 7.3 percent broadband connection rate.[108]
- Both DSL and cable modem service are available to more than 32 percent of the people in metropolitan areas with a population of 2.5 million or more; only 8 percent of rural areas have availability to both broadband services.[109]

On the positive side, though, the number of sparsely populated zip codes with broadband users increased by 69 percent, compared to an increase of 4 percent for the most densely populated zip codes.[110]

One of the major reasons large portions of the populations do not have access to high-speed Internet access is due to the physical limitations of broadband service. Many cable television systems are not yet upgraded to provide two-way Internet service via their network of coaxial cables, and DSL is only available in a three-mile radius of a telephone central switching station.[111]

Yet there are at least two emerging technologies that hope to fill in the gaps in the map where present broadband service does not or cannot reach. The first is a fixed wireless system known as MMDS in which users have a stationary digital transceiver pointed toward a radio transmission tower to gain high-speed Internet access.[112] In theory, every home and business in a thirty-five-mile radius with a line of sight to a radio transmission tower could have broadband access, thereby overcoming the physical shortcomings of cable and DSL service.[113] The other emerging technology is satellite-delivered, high-speed Internet access. Like MMDS, the satellite service does not rely on landlines and therefore can reach even the most isolated location. The company Starband, a leader in this field, pioneered their service to one of the most affected groups of the digital divide, Native Americans, by providing satellite-fed broadband access to remote Indian reservations—even at the bottom of the Grand Canyon.[114] However, until these emerging technologies mature and enter the mainstream, the fact remains that there is still a considerable gap between with those with high-speed Internet access and those without.

Access to Computers and Internet Devices

As outlined earlier, there are gaps along racial, economic, and education lines when it comes to access to Internet-ready computers at present. Critics of the digital divide often dismiss these gaps. Mark Lloyd best expressed this contrary school of thought by saying, "Internet-ready computers can now be bought for less than $300. And for those unwilling or unable to make this small purchase, they will have access to the Internet at work, or at school, or at a public library, or a community technology center. So what's the problem?"[115]

The problem, Mr. Lloyd, is the future. As technology evolves, the Internet will move away from the exclusive domain of personal computers into a wide range of devices and applications influencing almost every aspect of life. If there is a digital divide now with personal computers and the Internet, how huge of a gap will there be in the future? In five years, will we be debating the "digital chasm"?

It is predicted that there will be three main "emerging forces" involving the Internet: information appliances, digitally delivered services, and an omnipresent information technology infrastructure.[116] Information appliances will be anything with a computer chip and the ability to connect to the Internet: everything from the personal computers to pagers to Web-enabled cell phones to cars that communicate to the dealership about maintenance to "smart" refrigerators that tell you the milk has gone bad.[117] Literally billions of information appliances are foreseen,[118] so the current digital divide can be expected to grow exponentially as this technology spreads.

The second emerging force is digitally delivered services, or "e-services."[119] E-services will take any process or any asset that can be digitized and deliver it over the Internet.[120] Entire chains of transactions like global virtual learning and supply chain management will be electronically brokered.[121] If today there are large chunks of the population who do not have the access or ability to compose a simple e-mail, how will they fare in a few years when most of the economy and bureaucracy are e-services?

The third emerging force is the always-on computing and IT infra-structure to support the deluge of transactions of e-services.[122] This infrastructure will be so immensely powerful and pervasive that it will dwarf today's concept of the Internet. It is proclaimed that this infrastructure will "be as available and reliable as tap water."[123] If this metaphor is extended, it is not hard to imagine how divided society will be if large sections of the population not only do not have running water, but do not even know how to turn on a faucet.

Access to Usable Content

Underlying the problem of who has access to the Internet is the question of whether there is anything in the Internet of real value. There might be millions of websites containing billions of bits of information, but is any of it worthwhile? Yes, posting your resume, planning a vacation, buying a Christmas gift, and tracking your mutual funds are all worthwhile online activities . . . but worthwhile to whom? As the above examples indicate, the bulk of online content is geared to White, middle-class Americans—which means that the Internet's vast yet homogenized content is not as relevant and usable to the entire population as it should be.[124]

So not only is there a digital divide, there is also a "content divide." According to a University of Massachusetts study, 25 percent of people earning less than $40,000 a year would use Internet banking, but only 3 percent would use the Internet to find out about community events and neighborhood issues.[125] Why? Because of an absence of Internet content geared to their needs, such as affordable housing and day care.[126]

A look at the Internet habits of low-income users shows the starkness of the content divide. A 2000 study by Media Metrix found that the most popular Internet destination for those in the $25,000 household income bracket was a site called Valueplay.com, a free service that pays members when they go online.[127] Alas, as with many dot.com services, this site is not operational as of 2002. The second most popular site for this income group was DesktopDollars.com, a free incentive site that awards members for online transactions.[128]

In and of itself, there is nothing wrong with low-income users seeing freebies and rewards as the Internet's most valuable content, as long as this is not the only reason to go online. However, due to lower economic growth and shortage of ad revenues, the future of these sites is uncertain. "The Internet used to be a little like a 1968 Haight-Ashbury commune, where essentially everything was free," says Charles Ardai, chief executive of Juno Online Services. "Now," he says, "it's becoming more like Manhattan in 2001, where you have to pay for the things that you most want to do."[129] As their most attractive content (free offers and incentives) quickly disappears (replaced, ironically, by exactly what they cannot afford, pay services), low-income users fall headfirst into the Internet's content divide.

The content divide was best explored by a 2000 study from The Children's Partnership. This study identified four major types of "Internet barriers" in online content: lack of local information, literacy barriers, language barriers, and lack of cultural diversity.[130] The study found that an estimated 21 million Americans are underserved by lack of local online content, 44 million due to literacy barriers, 32 million because of language barriers, and 26 million due to the lack of culturally diverse content.[131] Since many are affected by a multiple of these factors, this meant a total of at least 50 million Americans are poorly served by the Internet because of a dearth of online content that targets the needs of people with low incomes and those with limited English abilities.[132]

This study examined 1,000 of the most popular websites and found that only 1 percent of the sites could be easily read by the 44 million Americans who read below the average literacy level.[133] The problem lies in the fact that the majority of the content is in text and graphics as opposed to the easier-to-understand sound and video.[134] Furthermore, while 32 million Americans' primary language is not English, 87 percent of the websites are in English.[135] Only 2 percent of the Web's most popular sites targeted Americans who do not speak English as their first language.[136]

Clearly, it is vital not only to provide equal access to the Internet, but to also provide equal access to relevant information online. To accomplish this goal, more emphasis needs to be placed on content for people with low incomes and limited English—for example, local job listings including jobs requiring entry-level skills, preparation for securing a high school equivalency degree, online translation tools, and cultural exploration and development.[137]

Employment

The U.S. Bureau of Labor Statistics has projected that over the decade ending in 2008, the United States will need almost 1.7 million additional computer engineers, programmers, and analysts.[138] These skilled positions generally require a four-year undergraduate degree and, in many cases, advanced training or a graduate degree.[139] The need for these skilled positions is growing even as the number of American college graduates with high-tech degrees is falling: 207,056 high-tech degrees were awarded in 1997, down 2 percent since 1990.[140]

Statistics show that those Americans who do earn university degrees in information technology (IT) related fields are predominantly White and male. Men earn approximately 85 percent of bachelor's degrees, 74.5 percent of master's degrees, and 88 percent of IT-related doctoral degrees.[141] Looking at the discipline of computer science as an example, women only earn approximately 27 percent of the bachelor's and master's degrees and 15 percent of the doctoral degrees for this field.[142] In addition, women in university computer science and computer engineering departments hold only 16 percent of assistant, 12 percent of associate, and 9 percent of full faculty positions.[143]

Minorities are also noticeably underrepresented in high-tech education. White non-Hispanics earn approximately 60 percent of bachelor's degrees, 29.5 percent of master's degrees, and 38 percent of doctoral IT-related degrees.[144] While on the surface these number might not appear overwhelming, it must be noted that these statistics are skewed because of the large number of international students awarded IT-related degrees from American colleges and universities.[145] For example, approximately 55 percent of master's and 48.5 percent of doctoral IT-related degrees awarded from American colleges and universities are earned by international students.[146]

Again, to use computer science as an example of the underrepresentation of minorities in IT-related fields:

- African Americans account for approximately 12 percent of the U.S. population, yet earn 11.17 percent of the bachelor's degrees, 5.38 percent of the master's degrees, and 1.78 percent of the doctoral degrees in computer science.[147]
- In the years 1990 to 1997, a total of sixty-six African Americans earned Ph.D. degrees in computer science, translating to an average of only 9.4 per year.[148]
- Hispanics account for approximately 10.4 percent of the U.S. population, yet earn 5.84 percent of the bachelor's degrees, 3.07 percent of the master's degrees, and 0.97 percent of the doctoral degrees in computer science.[149]

- In the years 1990 to 1997, a total of 123 Hispanics earned Ph.D. degrees in computer science, translating to an average of 17.6 per year.[150]
- Native Americans account for approximately 0.7 percent of the U.S. population, yet earn 0.49 percent of the bachelor's degrees, 0.25 percent of the master's degrees, and 0.00 percent of the doctoral degrees in computer science.[151]
- In the years 1990 to 1997, a total of six Native Americans earned Ph.D. degrees in computer science, translating to an average of less than one per year.[152]

This underrepresentation of women and minorities in IT-related studies manifests itself in lower employment in the IT sector.

- While African Americans constitute 10 percent of America's workforce, they only hold 5 percent of the economy's IT jobs.[153]
- While Hispanics make up 9 percent of America's workforce, they hold only 4 percent of the economy's IT jobs.[154]
- Women, half of America's workforce, hold only 20 percent of the economy's IT jobs.[155]

Despite the IT employment boom projected in the near future and the current glaring underrepresentation of women and minorities in IT studies, many policymakers are not focusing on nurturing the next generation of technology professionals—at least, not from the domestic labor pool. Instead, lawmakers are looking abroad. They favor the "H-1B visa" as the preferred method of filling high-tech positions.[156] Under the H-1B visa, high-tech workers from countries like India, China, and Taiwan are "invited" into the United States to fill these positions in American industry.[157] While not all H-1B visa holders are IT workers, the majority (60 percent) is.[158] This translates to over 70,000 IT jobs, the equivalent of 28 percent of the annual demand for IT workers with at least a bachelor's degree.[159]

Both Republicans and Democrats in Congress are pushing for legislation to double the current annual limit of 115,000 H-1B visas.[160] While some of these foreign workers do become naturalized American citizens, the majority does not, causing a "brain-drain" as they are forced by U.S. immigration law to return to their home country after their visas expire.

So the problem is three-fold. First, women and minorities are grossly underrepresented in information technology training and employment.

Second, the training and employment of the next generation of American high-tech workers is being sidestepped in favor of cheaper foreign labor. And third, almost as soon as these foreign workers mature into seasoned professionals, they are ushered back out of the country, leaving wide gaps in experience in the high-tech work force.

THE DIGITAL DIVIDE AND U.S. TARGET GROUPS

> Our findings, like those of the Department of Commerce, show greater home usage of the Internet by more highly educated and wealthier individuals. In particular, we found that compared with the general U.S. population, Internet users were more likely to be white and well educated and to have higher-than-average incomes.[161]

As the above quote states, the digital divide exists along demographic fault lines in the United States in 2001. Now that the various points in the digital divide debate have been addressed in the preceding sections, let us discuss the impact of the digital divide on specific target groups in the United States:

1. Low-income citizens
2. Racial and ethnic minorities
3. Rural communities
4. Seniors
5. The disabled
6. Women

Low-Income Citizens

Today, Americans at every income level are connecting to the Internet at far higher rates from their homes, particularly at the middle-income levels (figure 1.3). Internet access among households earning $35,000 to $49,000 rose from 29.0 percent in December 1998 to 46.1 percent in August 2000.[162] Now more than two-thirds of all households earning more than $50,000 have Internet connections (60.9 percent for households earning $50,000 to $74,999 and 77.7 percent for households earning above $75,000).[163] With this as background, households earning less than $25,000 in 1999 amounted to 7.9 percent of the total American Internet popula-

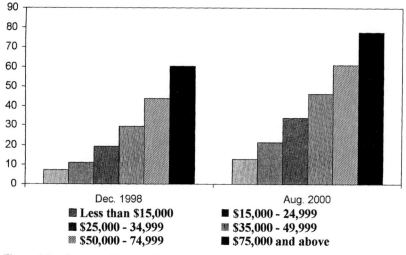

Figure 1.3.   *Percent of households with Internet access, by income level.*

tion; in 2000, that figure had grown to 9.7 percent.[164] Although these low-income households represent the fastest growing group of Internet users, they represent 32.1 percent of the total U.S. population,[165] yet they account for less than 10 percent of American households using the Internet.[166]

A huge reason for this anomaly is the gap in computer ownership between low-income households and middle- and upper-class families.

- Only 25 percent of families making less than $30,000 a year own a computer as opposed to 80 percent of households earning more than $100,000.[167]
- Only 22 percent of children in families with an annual income of less than $20,000 have access to a home computer, compared to 91 percent of children in families with incomes of more than $75,000.[168]

Looking beyond household computer and Internet access to general access (work, school, etc.), it is clear low-income individuals lag far behind other socioeconomic groups.

- Only 35 percent of adults in the low-income bracket have Internet access, compared to 53 percent in the lower-middle bracket, 79 percent in the upper-middle bracket, and 83 percent in the top bracket.[169]

- Non-Internet users are also less likely to be employed than Internet users; 42 percent of those not online have full-time jobs and 9 percent have part-time jobs, compared to 66 percent of Internet users who have full-time jobs and 14 percent who have part-time jobs.[170]
- At incomes below $15,000, Hispanics and African Americans are particularly unlikely to have Internet access (5.2 percent and 6.4 percent, respectively).[171]

Although the statistics on growing Internet use by low-income households are encouraging, a wary eye must be focused on the future. The Office of Management and Budget states that in the immediate future up to 75 percent of all transactions between individuals and the government (including those most important to low-income families like delivery of food stamps, Social Security benefits, and Medicaid information) will take place electronically.[172] Thus, the huge numbers of low-income households without technology skills and/or Internet access will be at a marked disadvantage.[173]

More importantly, the digital divide threatens to perpetuate the "old poverty" as low-income people who lack access to information technology are denied the opportunities to acquire the knowledge and skills necessary to function in the digital economy.[174] Therefore, they remain unemployed or confined to low-paying, menial jobs.[175]

As noted earlier, this leads many to believe that the digital divide is truly an economic and not a technology issue. In the words of *San Francisco Chronicle* writer Mark Simon, "If you want to close the digital divide, pay a decent wage that frees parents to concern themselves with technology and learning. . . . It's not enough to get computers in the hands of the technology have-nots, if both parents are working 16-hour days trying to eke out a living."[176]

Racial and Ethnic Minorities

When the digital divide is drawn along racial and ethnic lines, many fear that the digital divide is really "cybersegregation."[177] Although this section will show that there is a racial and ethnic component of the digital divide, not all minorities are on the wrong side of the divide.

- Asian Americans and Pacific Islanders have the highest level of home Internet access at 56.8 percent, compared to a national rate of 41.5 percent.[178]

- In the lowest income bracket (under $15,000), 33.2 percent of Asian Americans and Pacific Islanders have Internet access and 39.4 percent own a computer.[179]
- Approximately 60 percent of Chinese American households have a home Internet connection.[180]
- Ninety-seven percent of Chinese American Internet users own a home computer.[181]
- Asian Americans account for 3.4 percent of the total U.S. population, yet earn 10.57 percent of the bachelor's degrees, 19.2 percent of the master's degrees, and 22.37 percent of the doctoral degrees conferred in computer science in the United States.[182]

But for the nation's African American, Hispanic, and Native American populations, the digital divide is still an obstacle to parity.

African Americans

The divide between Internet access rates for African American households and the national average rate was 18.0 percentage points in August 2000 (a 23.5 percent penetration rate for African American households, compared to 41.5 percent for households nationally).[183] This divide is 3.0 percentage points wider than the 15.0 percentage-point gap that existed in December 1998.[184]

For individuals, while about a third of the U.S. population uses the Internet at home, only 18.9 percent of African Americans use the Internet at home.[185] Of the online African American population, just over 70 percent have home Internet access, compared to 84 percent of online Whites.[186]

This pattern holds true for African American children and teens: 23 percent of African American parents report that their children use the

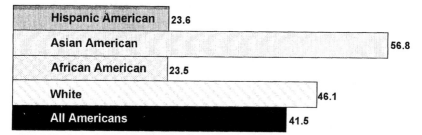

Figure 1.4.   *Percent of households with Internet access, based on race and ethnicity.*

Internet, compared to 57 percent of White parents.[187] And, like the African American population as whole, home Internet access lags for African American children: 80 percent of African American children age nine to seventeen who use the Internet access it from school, compared to only 16 percent who access it from home.[188]

Differences in education levels and income and do not fully explain this component of the digital divide. Estimates of what Internet access rates for African American and Hispanic American households would have been if they had incomes and education levels as high as the nation as a whole show that education and income account for about one-half of the differences.[189] Yet there does appear to be a correlation to household location: African American households in rural areas are 40 percent less likely to access the Internet than the average African American household.[190]

With regard to computer ownership, the divide remains large, although it has stabilized. The August 2000 computer ownership divide between African American households and the national average rate was 18.4 percentage points (a 32.6 percent penetration rate for African American households, compared to 51.0 percent for households nationally).[191] Statistically, this computer ownership gap is no different from the one that existed in December 1998.[192] And like Internet access, rural African Americans trail in computer ownership: they are 20 percent less likely to own a home computer than the average African American household.[193]

But there are some encouraging signs:

- The Internet's African American population practically doubled in 1999 as 3.5 million African Americans went online for the first time[194]—over a quarter of the new users going online in the past six months.[195]
- The gap between Whites and African Americans might shrink in the future as 46 percent of African Americans who are not currently online say that will "probably or definitely" go online in the future; only 40 percent of Whites say the same thing.[196]
- African American households' total spending on computers has increased 143 percent, from $553 million to $1.35 billion, while comparable spending by White households has only increased 10 percent.[197] In specifics, computer hardware purchases by African Americans more than tripled in one year, from $354 million to

$1.05 billion, and software purchases leaped more than 50 percent, from $137 million to $214 million.[198]

- Spending by African Americans for home Internet access increased from $10 million in 1996 to $62 million in 1997, and then to $89 million in 1998.[199]

Hispanic Americans

For Hispanic American households, the difference in Internet penetration between their rate and the national average rate was 17.9 percentage points in August 2000 (a 23.6 percent penetration rate for Hispanic American households, compared to 41.5 percent for households nationally).[200] This gap is 4.3 percentage points wider than the 13.6 percentage point gap that existed in December 1998.[201]

For individuals, while nearly a third of the U.S. population uses the Internet at home, only 16.1 percent of Hispanic Americans do so.[202]

And, like African Americans, differences in educational levels and income do not fully explain this component of the digital divide. Estimates of what Internet access rates for Hispanic American households would have been if they had incomes and education levels as high as the nation as a whole show that education and income account for about one-half of the differences.[203]

And, again like African Americans, the 17.3 percentage point difference between the share of Hispanic American households with a computer (33.7 percent) and the national average (51 percent) was not a statistically significant change from the December 1998 computer divide.[204]

Native Americans

For Native Americans and the digital divide, the three major factors are income, rural location, and a lack of basic telephone service.

- The per capita annual income for all Native Americans is only $8,234 and the per capita income for Native Americans living on reservations or trust lands is only $4,478.[205]
- Approximately half of the Native American population of 2,369,000 live in rural or semirural locations west of the Mississippi River.[206]

- Fifty-three percent of Native American homes on reservations do not have a telephone.[207] For example, 83.9 percent of the homes on the San Carlos Reservation in Arizona and 81.6 percent of the homes on the Navajo Reservation and Trust Lands in Arizona, New Mexico, and Utah do not have telephones.[208] As a comparison, only 5 percent of homes in the United States and 9 percent of homes in rural areas of the United States do not have a telephone.[209]

In light of Native American's shockingly low incomes and the appalling state of basic telephone service on reservations, it should be no surprise that Native Americans' computer and Internet access rates are so lagging.

- In the areas where there is phone service, household computer ownership accompanied with Internet access is no greater than 15 percent.[210]
- Of the 185 tribal schools and colleges supported by the Bureau of Indian Affairs, only 76 are connected to the Internet.[211]

In a perfect example of the universal service ideal, in 2000, President Clinton initiated a plan to bring basic telephone service to at least some of the unconnected Native Americans.[212] The plan calls for a 0.4 percent increase in long-distance rates to generate $17 million to subsidize basic phones service for 300,000 Native Americans.[213]

Rural Communities

The status of the digital divide in rural areas is a mix of good and bad news.

- Internet access leaped for rural households from 22.2 percent in 1998 to 38.9 percent in 2000 (compared to the national rate of 41.5 percent).[214]
- Internet access for rural households with an income below $15,000 rose from 4.6 percent to 11.3 percent between 1998 and 2000.[215]
- But the Internet access rate for rural households with an income of $50,000 to $74,999 is 59.5 percent (up over 20 percentage points since 1998); and the Internet access rate for rural households with

an income of $75,000 and above is 76.6 percent (up almost 23 percentage points since 1998).[216]

- Of all household types, nonfamily (single or unmarried) households in rural areas are the least likely to have Internet access (20.2 percent).[217]
- For racial and ethnic groups, there is a "significantly lower" Internet penetration rate between urban and rural areas: 48.3 percent for Whites in urban areas compared to 40.9 percent for Whites in rural areas; 24 percent for African Americans in urban areas compared to 19.9 percent for African Americans in rural areas; 23.9 percent for Hispanics in urban areas compared to 19.9 percent for Hispanics in rural areas.[218]
- Forty-two percent of rural residents do not use computers, compared to 34 percent of suburbanites and 31 percent of those living in urban areas.[219]
- Eighty percent of public libraries in urban areas have public Internet access, compared to 66 percent of public libraries in rural areas.[220]

So, despite rural areas' near parity in Internet access compared to the nation as whole, gaps still persist. Notably, the divide in Internet access between the poorest and wealthiest rural households and the disparity

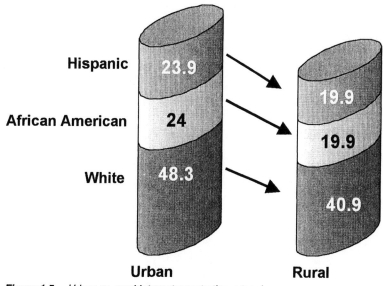

Figure 1.5.   *Urban vs. rural Internet penetration rates, by group.*

among racial and ethnic groups in urban and rural communities are clear examples of the current rural digital divide.

Moreover, rural communities are still faced with physical and geographic barriers to Internet access. While there are many Internet service providers (ISPs) with local points-of-presence (and, thus local access numbers for dial-up service) competing for the business of suburban and urban communities, rural residents often do not have this convenience.[221] For a large segment of the rural population, a long-distance call is necessary to access the Internet,[222] amounting to an added "rural tax" to the cost of Internet service.

This lack of local ISP service is a major stumbling block to closing the rural digital divide. Research done by Shane Greenstein of Northwestern University and Tom Downes of Tufts University shows that in 11 percent of all U.S. counties—home to 1 to 2 percent of the U.S. population—there was no local ISP.[223] While 92 percent of the nation has a competitive ISP market, 6 percent of U.S. residents living in sparsely populated rural areas have only a single ISP in their local calling area.[224] In rural areas where local Internet service does exist, most likely a local "mom-and-pop" ISP provides it.[225] It is estimated that it takes 200 subscriber households to make a rural "mom-and-pop" ISP economically viable and 1,000 to justify a local point-of-presence by a national ISP.[226] This makes it unlikely that any rural community with a population under 5,000 will get local service from a national ISP.[227]

In addition to dial-up access issues, rural communities also are often on the wrong side of the broadband digital divide. Broadband subscribers are present in 96 percent of the most densely populated zip codes yet in only 40 percent of zip codes with the lowest population densities.[228]

Furthermore:

- While cities have a 12.2 percent broadband connection rate (among households with Internet access), rural areas have only a 7.3 percent broadband connection rate.[229]
- Both DSL and cable modem service are available to more than 32 percent of the people in metropolitan areas with a population of 2.5 million or more; only 8 percent of rural areas have availability to both broadband services.[230]
- DSL broadband service is available in 56 percent of cities with populations of more than 100,000 compared to less than 5 percent in towns with populations under 10,000.[231]

- Cable modem broadband service is available in 65 percent of cities with a population of more than 250,000 compared to less than 5 percent in towns of 10,000 or less.[232]

Where broadband service is available, there is often a huge difference in cost for urban and rural users. As an example, businesses in rural Columbus County, North Carolina, spend an average of $21,000 a year for high-speed access as opposed to an average cost of $3,000 a year for businesses in the capital city of Raleigh.[233] In large part, this is due to the physical limitations of DSL service coupled with the geographical isolation of many rural residents. DSL service is only available to households within a three-mile radius of a main telephone switching station. In a highly urbanized state like New Jersey, the average distance between a customer and the nearest telephone switching station is 2.6 miles.[234] In a rural state like Wyoming, the average distance is twice as far and the cost to the phone company to reach the consumer is twice as high.[235]

The broadband divide poses the largest threat to rural communities. As Edwin Parker stated in *Closing the Digital Divide in Rural America*, "rural communities not connected to our emerging broadband network will suffer the same fate as many communities that were bypassed by the . . . railroad and Interstate highway system. The railroads and Interstates couldn't be everywhere so rural winners and losers were created. Similarly . . . [rural] communities left off the new broadband network will inevitably suffer economic decline."[236]

Seniors

For older Americans, the digital divide is still quite wide. Individuals fifty-five years old and older, regardless of income or educational level, are among the least likely to be computer and Internet users.[237] And while the numbers of seniors online has grown recently, these numbers closely parallel the overall increase of seniors in the general population,[238] which means that the actual percentage of seniors who access the Internet has only risen by 2 percent.[239]

The computer gap for seniors breaks down this way:

- Fifty-seven percent of Americans over age fifty do not use computers.[240]

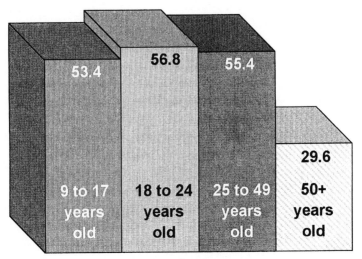

Figure 1.6. Percent using Internet, by age group.

- One-third of the entire noncomputer population in the United States are women over the age of fifty.[241]
- Only 27 percent of Americans over age sixty have access to a computer at work or home, compared to 78 percent of Americans under the age of thirty.[242]
- However, individuals over fifty years old were almost three times as likely to be Internet users if they were in the labor force than if they were not.[243]
- A thirty-year-old in a household earning $75,000 a year is 20 percent more likely to use a computer than a sixty-year-old in the same income bracket.[244]
- Twenty-eight percent of Americans over the age of fifty who have a college or graduate degree do not use a computer, compared to only 6 percent of those under thirty with a college or graduate degree.[245]

The statistics on Internet access for seniors reflect their disproportionately low computer use.

- Only 15 percent of Americans sixty-five and over have Internet access, compared to 75 percent of those between the ages of eighteen and twenty-nine.[246]
- Forty-one percent of Americans between fifty and sixty-four have Internet access, compared to 65 percent of those under age thirty.[247]

- Americans age fifty and above account for half of the entire non-online population.[55]
- The older the non-Internet user, the less likely he is to say he will access the Internet in the future; 44.3 percent of people "not likely" to access the Internet in the next year are greater than fifty-six years old.[249]

As outlined earlier, with services vital to senior citizens like Social Security and Medicaid moving to the Internet, the need to bridge the age-defined digital divide and provide seniors with the tools and training to gain access is critical.[250] Yet despite social myths to the contrary, the root problem is not that seniors are "technophobic."[251] According to a study cosponsored by Microsoft and the American Society on Aging, 82 percent of seniors believe technology literacy is essential for educational success, 75 percent feel that technology skills are important for enhanced or continued employability, and 52 percent think that technology is a key for independent living.[252]

Obviously, the majority of seniors knows the importance of technology and is ready to embrace it. The real issue is the lack of access to technology training for seniors. Seventy percent of seniors report that there are no "senior-friendly" technology training programs offered to them.[253]

The Disabled

There are 54 million people with disabilities in the United States, making the disabled the largest U.S. minority group at almost 20 percent of the general population.[254] For people with disabilities, who are often physically as well as socially isolated, information technology has a huge potential to increase their independence and broaden their lives.[255]

But, as Senator Tom Harkin said, "technology is a double-edged sword for people with disabilities. If the Internet and other technologies are accessible, they will offer . . . unprecedented opportunities for independence and self-sufficiency . . . but if they are not accessible, they will create new barriers."[256]

As the following statistics illustrate, a new barrier in the form of the digital divide is being thrown in front of people with disabilities.

- Only 24 percent of people with disabilities have a computer in their household.[257]

- Only 11.4 percent of people with disabilities have home Internet access and only 9.9 percent of people with disabilities use the Internet.[258]
- For people with disabilities age sixty-five and older, only 10.6 percent have a home computer and just 2.2 percent use the Internet.[259]
- Sixty percent of people with disabilities have never used a personal computer, compared to just fewer than 25 percent of those without a disability.[260]

A digital divide even exists within the disabled community. People who have impaired vision and problems with manual dexterity have even lower rates of Internet access and are less likely to use a computer regularly than people with hearing and mobility problems. This difference holds in the aggregate, as well as across age groups.[261]

For people with disabilities, the digital divide is not only about access, it is also about accessibility.[262] It is estimated that close to 90 percent of Web pages have accessibility problems for the disabled.[263] For example, the recent Graphics, Visualization, and Usability Center Survey of Internet Users found that approximately 4 percent of those online have some kind of visual disability,[264] meaning that websites that rely on text and graphic as opposed to audio pose an accessibility problem.

Congress has taken steps to improve Internet accessibility for the disabled—"building curb cuts on the Information Highway."[265] As mandated by Section 508 of the 1998 Workforce Investment Act, most

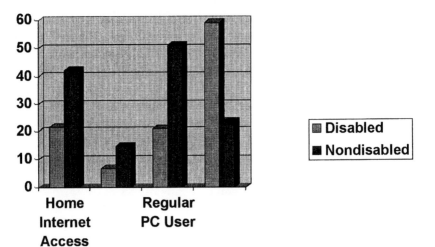

Figure 1.7. *Disability and the digital divide.*

federal government websites now must be accessible to people with disabilities.[266] Under the law, federal websites must be revised to ensure they are accessible to disabled people, including "users who have poor vision, blindness, or lack of color perception, users who are hard of hearing, users who have limited strength or lack of sensation, users with epilepsy, and users with language and learning disabilities."[267] To make federal websites accessible to the blind, the sites must be revised to "provide at least one mode that does not require vision"[268] by formatting all online information to be compatible with Braille and speech-synthesis devices.[269] To make federal websites accessible to those with hearing problems, streaming audio or audio files must be accompanied by simultaneous text.[270]

While these regulations go far to make important federal websites (Medicare, Social Security, etc.) more accessible to the disabled, they do nothing to remedy the accessibility problems the disabled face at the literally millions of private and corporate websites.

Women

Although the digital divide between men and women was quite pronounced several years ago, the "gender gap" has been erased . . . almost. Regrettably, several significant issues still remain that affect women and information technology.

First, the good news:

- Of the entire American online population, women now edge out men; 50.4 percent of American Internet users are female.[271]
- There is virtual parity in the Internet use rate of males (44.6 percent) and females (44.2 percent).[272]
- The Internet use rates for African American (30.5 percent) and Hispanic (24.7 percent) women are higher than those of African American men (27.9 percent) and Hispanic men (22.7 percent).[273]
- The Internet use rate for women aged eighteen to twenty-five is 59.6 percent, compared to 54.1 percent for men in the same age group.[274]
- Of women aged twenty-five to forty-nine in the labor force, 60.8 percent are Internet users, compared to 56.2 percent of men in the same group[275]
- Of women aged twenty-five to forty-nine not in the labor force, 42.6 percent are Internet users, compared to 28.6 percent of men in the same group.[276]

Despite all the encouraging signs, the digital divide still exists for women in certain racial, age, and household groups.

- The Internet use rate for Asian American women is 46.1 percent compared to 52.7 percent for Asian American men.[277]
- Of women fifty and older not in the labor force, 15.6 percent are Internet users, compared to 18.1 percent of men in the same group.[278]
- In single-parent families, 30.0 percent for female-headed households have Internet access, compared to 35.7 percent for male-headed households (60.6 percent of dual-parent households have Internet access).[279]
- In inner cities, only 22.8 percent of female-headed, single-parent households have Internet access.[280]

There are also indications that women's Internet access and use rates will plateau or even drop: in the non-online population, 56 percent of those who will "probably not go online" in the future are women, and 57 percent of those who will "never" go online are women.[281]

Perhaps the most telling and troubling aspect of the gender-based digital divide is the current and future role of women in America's technology-driven society and economy. Considering the statistics listed below, it is not hard to see why only approximately 20 percent of information technology professionals in the country are female.[282]

- Women earn only 15 percent of bachelor's, 25.5 percent of master's, and 12 percent of information technology-related doctoral degrees.[283]
- Women only earn approximately 27 percent of the bachelor's and master's degrees and 15 percent of computer science doctoral degrees;[284] computer science is the only academic field in which women's participation has actually decreased over time.[285]
- Women in university computer science and computer engineering departments hold only 16 percent of assistant, 12 percent of associate, and 9 percent of full faculty positions.[286]
- These trends do not appear likely to change in the foreseeable future: only 17 percent of high school computer science AP test takers are female.[287]

These facts point to an alarming trend that women are not equally represented in the ever-increasingly important realm of information technology. Thus, though women may be at close to an equal footing

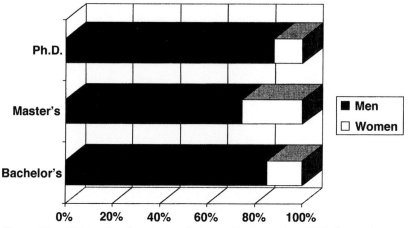

Figure 1.8.   *Higher education degrees in information technology fields, by gender.*

with men in terms of using technology, they are not mastering technology as men are.

NOTES

1. Ricardo Gomez, "The Hall of Mirrors: The Internet in Latin America," *Current History* 99, no. 634 (2000).

2. Andy Carvin, "Mind the Gap: The Digital Divide as the Civil Rights Issue of the New Millennium," *MultiMedia Schools,* January/February 2000.

3. Stephanie Ernst, "Bush, Gore Vow to Bridge the Digital Divide," *DiversityInc.com,* at www.diversityinc.com (accessed August 16, 2000).

4. Jamal Le Blanc, "Politics and the Digital Divide, Part 2: Governor Bush, The Republicans and the 'Digital Opportunity'," *Digital Divide Network,* at www.digitaldividenetwork.org/content/sections/index.cfm (accessed October 8, 2000).

5. "FCC Chief Raises Eyebrow at 'Digital Divide,'" *CNN.com,* at www9.cnn.com/2001/TECH/industry/02/07/fcc.chairman.ap/index.html (accessed February 7, 2001).

6. Speech given by Ms. Fiorina to the National Governor's Association, Washington, D.C., 27 February 2000.

7. Carvin, "Mind the Gap," *MultiMedia Schools.*

8. Alcide. L. Honore, "Finding the Digital Divide," Duke University, at www.duke.edu/~gronke/webofpolitics/projects/digitaldivide/index.htm (accessed March 2, 2001).

9. The Southern Growth Policy Board, "Creating a CyberSouth," September 2000.

10. The Southern Growth Policy Board, "Creating a CyberSouth."

11. National Telecommunications and Information Administration, "Fact Sheet: 'Digital Divide' Widening at Lower Income Levels," *Falling through the Net: Defining the Digital Divide* (Washington, D.C.: U.S. Dept. of Commerce, November 1999).

12. Daniel Gross, "The Digital Divide," *TheStreet.com*, at www.thestreet .com/comment/ballotdance/1142108.html (accessed October 26, 2000).

13. National Telecommunications and Information Administration, *Falling through the Net.*

14. National Telecommunications and Information Administration, *Falling through the Net.*

15. Gross, "The Digital Divide," *TheStreet.com.*

16. Ernst, "Bush, Gore Vow to Bridge the Digital Divide," *DiversityInc.com.*

17. Ernst, "Bush, Gore Vow to Bridge the Digital Divide," *DiversityInc.com.*

18. Employment Policy Foundation, "Computer Ownership and Internet Access: Opportunities for Workforce Development and Job Flexibility" (Washington, D.C.: Employment Policy Foundation, January 2001).

19. Federal Communication Commission, "Connecting the Globe: A Regulator's Guide to Building a Global Information Community" (Washington, D.C.: FCC, June 1999).

20. Federal Communication Commission, "Connecting the Globe."

21. National Academy of Sciences, "Fostering Research on the Economic and Social Impacts of Information Technology" at www.nap.edu/ readingroom/books/esi/ch2.html#22 (accessed March 1, 2001).

22. National Academy of Sciences, "Fostering Research on the Economic and Social Impacts of Information Technology."

23. National Academy of Sciences, "Fostering Research on the Economic and Social Impacts of Information Technology."

24. *Telecommunications Act of 1996*, SR. 652.

25. *Telecommunications Act of 1996*, SR. 652.

26. *Telecommunications Act of 1996*, SR. 652.

27. L. Jean Camp, "Universal Service in a Ubiquitous Digital Network" at ksghome.harvard.edu/~.jcamp.academic.ksg/inet.html#history (accessed March 1, 2001).

28. The Gartner Group, "A Report on the Digital Divide and Its Social and Economic Implications for Our Nation and Its Citizens" (Washington, D.C.: Gartner, October 2000).

29. The Bill & Melinda Gates Foundation, "The Digital Divide" at gatesfoundation.org/learning/digitaldivide.htm (accessed March 20, 2001).

30. Peter Martek, "Speakers Seek End to Digital Divide," *The Hartford Courant*, February 11, 2001.

31. Paul A. Greenberg, "Study: Digital Divide Not Race-Based," *E-Commerce Times*, April 17, 2000.

32. Carvin, "Mind the Gap," *MultiMedia Schools.*

33. Bosah Ebo, ed., *Cyberghetto or Cybertopia: Race, Class, and Gender on the Internet* (Westport, Conn.: Praeger, 1998).

34. Carvin, "Mind the Gap," *MultiMedia Schools*.

35. UCLA Center for Communication Policy, "The UCLA Internet Report: Surveying the Digital Future" (Los Angeles: University of Southern California, November 2000).

36. Mick Brady, "The Digital Divide Myth," *E-Commerce Times*, August 4, 2000.

37. Brady, "The Digital Divide Myth," *E-Commerce Times*.

38. Christy Mumford Jerding, "True Nature of 'Digital Divide' Divides Experts," *The Freedom Forum Online*, March 17, 2000.

39. Dan Richman, "Gate Rejects Idea of E-Utopia," *Seattle Post-Intelligencer*, October 19, 2000.

40. Gully.com, "Chairman Mike and the Digital Divide" at www.thegully .com/essays/US/politics_2001/010212powell_fcc.html (accessed February 12, 2001).

41. Adam Clayton Powell III, "Falling for the Gap: Whatever Happened to the Digital Divide?" *Reason Online*, November 1999.

42. Ekaterina Walsh, "The Truth about the Digital Divide," Forrester Research, April 2000.

43. Barbara Humes, "Understanding Information Literacy," Office of Educational Research, National Institute on Postsecondary Education, Libraries, and Lifelong Learning (Washington, D.C.: U.S. Department of Education, September 1999).

44. The Southern Growth Policy Board, "Creating a CyberSouth."

45. NUA Internet Surveys, at www.nua.com (accessed October 3, 2000).

46. Humes, "Understanding Information Literacy."

47. Elizabeth Kiggen, "Clinton Proclaims Explosive Net Progress," *NewsFactor Network*, at www.newsfactor.com/perl/story/6790.html (accessed March 12, 2001).

48. UCLA Center for Communication Policy, "The UCLA Internet Report: Surveying the Digital Future,"

49. UCLA Center for Communication Policy, "The UCLA Internet Report: Surveying the Digital Future."

50. UCLA Center for Communication Policy, "The UCLA Internet Report: Surveying the Digital Future."

51. Edwin B. Parker, "Closing the Digital Divide in Rural America," *Telecommunications Policy Online*, May 2000.

52. Eileen Alt Powell, "More and More Americans Filing Taxes Online," *Nando Times*, at archive.nandotimes.com/technology/story/0,1643,500461290 -500703024-503836034-0,00.html (accessed March 15, 2001).

53. Booz, Allen, and Hamilton, "Achieving Universal Access" at www.number-10.gov.uk/default.asp?PageID=1203 (accessed March 15, 2001).

54. Global Internet Project, "The Emergence of a Networked World: Commerce, Society and the Future of the Internet" at www.gip.org/publications/papers/gip2e.asp (accessed March 12, 2001).

55. Doug Brown, "Cancer Institute Seeks to Bridge Divide," *Inter@ctive Week*, at www.zdnet.com/zdnn/stories/news/0,4586,2585261,00.html (accessed March 21, 2001).

56. Global Internet Project, "The Emergence of a Networked World."

57. Global Internet Project, "The Emergence of a Networked World."

58. "National Public Radio/Kaiser Family Foundation/Kennedy School of Government Survey of Americans on Technology," February 2000.

59. U.S. Department of Commerce, "The Emerging Digital Economy" at www.ecommerce.gov/danc1.htm (accessed November 1, 2000).

60. University of Texas Center for Research in Economic Commerce, "Internet Indicators" (University of Texas, 1999).

61. NUA Internet Surveys, "Internet Supports 3 Million U.S. Jobs" at www.nua.com (accessed January 15, 2001).

62. Robert Atkinson and Randolph Court, "The New Economy Index," The Progressive Policy Institute (Washington, D.C., 1999).

63. *The Internet Economy Indicators* at www.internetindicators.com/internetindic.html (accessed March 16, 2001).

64. *The Internet Economy Indicators.*

65. NUA Internet Surveys, "Internet Supports 3 Million U.S. Jobs."

66. Michael Pastore "Search Engines, Browsers Still Confusing Many Web Users" at cyberatlas.internet.com/big_picture/traffic_patterns/article/0,,5931_588851,00.html (accessed February 14, 2001).

67. "High-Speed Access Just a Dream for Many Americans," *CyberAtlas: The Web Marketers Guide to Online Facts*, August 15, 2000.

68. "High-Speed Access Just a Dream for Many Americans," *CyberAtlas.*

69. "Search Engines, Browsers Still Confusing Many Web Users."

70. Blake Bailey, "The Private Sector Is Closing the Digital Divide: Brief Analysis No. 331," National Center for Policy Analysis (Washington, D.C.: August 2000).

71. Deroy Murdock, "Digital Divide? What Digital Divide?" *The Cato Institute* at www.cato.org/dailys/06-16-00.html (accessed March 1, 2001).

72. "Should Schools Be Wired to the Internet?" *Time Magazine* 151, no. 20 (May 25, 1998).

73. Jim Geraghty, "The Digital Divide and the Paper Divide," *Policy.com* at www.policy.com/news/dig_div.htm (accessed March 4, 2001).

74. NUA Internet Surveys, "Sixty Percent of Americans Are Online" at www.nua.ie/surveys/index.cgi?f=VS&art_id=905356461&rel=true (accessed February 15, 2001).

75. NUA Internet Surveys, "Sixty Percent of Americans are Online."

76. Pew Internet Project, "Who's Not Online?" (Washington, D.C.: September 2000).

77. Pew Internet Project, "Who's Not Online?"

78. "Search Engines, Browsers Still Confusing Many Web Users."

79. "Search Engines, Browsers Still Confusing Many Web Users."

80. "Search Engines, Browsers Still Confusing Many Web Users."

81. Jay Lyman, "Study: Urbanites Want Greater Net Access," *NewsFactor Network*, at www.newsfactor.com/perl/story/6730.html (accessed March 21, 2001).

82. Stanford Institute for the Quantitative Study of Society, "SIQSS Internet Study" (Stanford University, February 2000).

83. UCLA Center for Communication Policy, "The UCLA Internet Report: Surveying the Digital Future."

84. Pew Internet Project, "Internet Tracking Report" (Washington, D.C.: February 2001).

85. "High-Speed Access Just a Dream for Many Americans," *CyberAtlas*.

86. "High-Speed Access Just a Dream for Many Americans," *CyberAtlas*.

87. "High-Speed Access Just a Dream for Many Americans," *CyberAtlas*.

88. "High-Speed Access Just a Dream for Many Americans," *CyberAtlas*.

89. "High-Speed Access Just a Dream for Many Americans," *CyberAtlas*.

90. "High-Speed Access Just a Dream for Many Americans," *CyberAtlas*.

91. "High-Speed Access Just a Dream for Many Americans," *CyberAtlas*.

92. "High-Speed Access Just a Dream for Many Americans," *CyberAtlas*.

93. Blake Bailey, "The Private Sector Is Closing the Digital Divide: Brief Analysis No. 331" (Washington, D.C.: National Center for Policy Analysis, August 2000).

94. "Federal Communications Commission Report on Deployment of High-Speed Internet" (Washington, D.C.: Federal Communications Commission, October 2000).

95. National Telecommunications and Information Administration, *Falling through the Net: Toward Digital Inclusion* (Washington, D.C.: U.S. Dept. of Commerce, October 2000).

96. Federal Communications Commission, "Second 706 Report on the Availability of High-Speed and Advanced Telecommunications Services" (Washington, D.C.: August 2000).

97. "Federal Communications Commission Report on Deployment of High-Speed Internet."

98. Neil Irwin, "FCC Cites a Higher-Speed Digital Divide," *Washington Post*, August 4, 2000.

99. Neil Irwin, "FCC Cites a Higher-Speed Digital Divide."

100. "Federal Communications Commission Report on Deployment of High-Speed Internet."

101. National Telecommunications and Information Administration, *Falling through the Net: Toward Digital Inclusion*.

102. "Characteristics and Choices of Internet Users" (Washington, D.C.: General Accounting Office, February 2001).

103. "Characteristics and Choices of Internet Users."

104. "Characteristics and Choices of Internet Users."

105. "Characteristics and Choices of Internet Users."

106. "Characteristics and Choices of Internet Users."

107. "Federal Communications Commission Report on Deployment of High-Speed Internet."

108. "Federal Communications Commission Report on Deployment of High-Speed Internet."

109. "Characteristics and Choices of Internet Users."

110. "Federal Communications Commission Report on Deployment of High-Speed Internet."

111. Peter S. Goodman, "Dishing Up a New Link to the Internet," *Washington Post*, November 6, 2000.

112. Patricia Fusco, "Sprint's Wireless Technology Rocks the Monopoly," *Internetnews.com* at www.news.com/news/internet/0304.htm (accessed March 4, 2001).

113. Patricia Fusco, "Sprint's Wireless Technology Rocks the Monopoly."

114. Peter S. Goodman, "Dishing Up a New Link to the Internet."

115. Mark Lloyd, "Understanding the Digital Divide" (speech at Audrey Cohen College, July 10, 2000).

116. Carly Fiorina, "Cyberspace and the American Dream VII" (speech at *Aspen Summit 2000* Aspen, Colorado, August 2000).

117. Fiorina, "Cyberspace and the American Dream VII."

118. Fiorina, "Cyberspace and the American Dream VII."

119. Fiorina, "Cyberspace and the American Dream VII."

120. Fiorina, "Cyberspace and the American Dream VII."

121. Fiorina, "Cyberspace and the American Dream VII."

122. Fiorina, "Cyberspace and the American Dream VII."

123. Fiorina, "Cyberspace and the American Dream VII."

124. Dara O'Neil and Jim Demmers, "Leavers and Takers: Alternative Perspectives on Universal Access to Telecommunications Technologies," paper presented to the 1999 Conference for the Society for Philosophy and Technology, San Jose State University, California, July 1999).

125. Jay Lyman, "Study: Urbanites Want Greater Net Access," *NewsFactor Network*, at www.newsfactor.com/perl/story/6730.html (accessed March 21, 2001).

126. Jay Lyman, "Study: Urbanites Want Greater Net Access."

127. Louise Rosen, "The Digital Divide Is Narrowing," *UpsideToday*, August 21, 2000.

128. Rosen, "The Digital Divide Is Narrowing."

129. David Streitfeld and Ariana Eunjung Cha, "Dot-Coms Pull Back On Internet Freebies," *Washington Post*, March 18, 2001.

130. The Children's Partnership, "Online Content for Low-Income and Underserved Americans: The Digital Divide's New Frontier" (New York: July 2000).

131. The Children's Partnership, "Online Content for Low-Income and Underserved Americans."

132. The Children's Partnership, "Online Content for Low-Income and Underserved Americans."

133. The Children's Partnership, "Online Content for Low-Income and Underserved Americans."

134. The Children's Partnership, "Online Content for Low-Income and Underserved Americans."

135. The Children's Partnership, "Online Content for Low-Income and Underserved Americans."

136. The Children's Partnership, "Online Content for Low-Income and Underserved Americans."

137. The Children's Partnership, "Online Content for Low-Income and Underserved Americans."

138. Marjorie Valbruin, "Groups Says Visas Widen Digital Divide," *The Wall Street Journal*, July 7, 2000.

139. U.S. Department of Commerce, "The Emerging Digital Economy" at www.ecommerce.gov/danc1.htm (accessed November 1, 2000).

140. Valbruin, "Groups Says Visas Widen Digital Divide," *The Wall Street Journal*.

141. Kade Twist, "Disparities along the Information Age Career Path," *The Benton Foundation* at www.digitaldividenetwork.org/content/sections/index.cfm?key=5 (accessed March 1, 2001).

142. Doris L. Carver, "Research Foundations for Improving the Representations of Women in the Information Technology Workforce" (Louisiana State University: November 1999).

143. Carver, "Research Foundations for Improving the Representations of Women in the Information Technology Workforce."

144. Twist, "Disparities along the Information Age Career Path," *The Benton Foundation*.

145. Twist, "Disparities along the Information Age Career Path," *The Benton Foundation*.

146. Twist, "Disparities along the Information Age Career Path," *The Benton Foundation*.

147. Oscar N. Garcia, "Researching Foundations on Successful Participation of Underrepresented Minorities in Information Technology" (Wright University, November 1999).

148. Garcia, "Researching Foundations on Successful Participation of Underrepresented Minorities in Information Technology."

149. Garcia, "Researching Foundations on Successful Participation of Underrepresented Minorities in Information Technology."

150. Garcia, "Researching Foundations on Successful Participation of Underrepresented Minorities in Information Technology."

151. Garcia, "Researching Foundations on Successful Participation of Underrepresented Minorities in Information Technology."

152. Garcia, "Researching Foundations on Successful Participation of Underrepresented Minorities in Information Technology."

153. John Simons, "Cheap Computers Bridge Digital Divide," *The Wall Street Journal*, at www.newamerica.net/articles/Simons/js-WallstreetJournal1-27-00.htm (accessed March 1, 2001).

154. Simons, "Cheap Computers Bridge Digital Divide," *The Wall Street Journal*.

155. American Association of University Women Educational Foundation Research, "Tech-Savvy: Educating Girls in the New Computer Age" (Washington, D.C.: AAUW, 2000).

156. Valbruin, "Groups Says Visas Widen Digital Divide," *The Wall Street Journal*.

157. Valbruin, "Groups Says Visas Widen Digital Divide," *The Wall Street Journal*.

158. "Meeting Workforce Demands in the Digital Economy," *The Benton Foundation* at www.digitaldividenetwork.org/content/sections/index.cfm?key=7 (accessed March 1, 2000).

159. "Meeting Workforce Demands in the Digital Economy," *The Benton Foundation*.

160. Valbruin, "Groups Says Visas Widen Digital Divide," *The Wall Street Journal*.

161. "Characteristics and Choices of Internet Users."

162. National Telecommunications and Information Administration, *Falling through the Net: Toward Digital Inclusion*.

163. National Telecommunications and Information Administration, *Falling through the Net: Toward Digital Inclusion*.

164. Louise Rosen, "The Digital Divide Is Narrowing."

165. "The Dollar Divide," *The Benton Foundation* at www.digitaldividenetwork .org/content/sections/index.cfm?key=5 (accessed March 1, 2000).

166. "Low Income Families Increase Internet Use," *San Francisco Chronicle*, August 21, 2000.

167. "Losing Ground Bit by Bit: Low-Income Communities in the Information Age," *The Benton Foundation*, at www.digitaldividenetwork.org/content/sections/index.cfm?key=3 (accessed March 1, 2000).

168. Tamar Lewin, "Children's Computer Use Grows, But Gaps Persist, Study Says," *The New York Times*, at www.nytimes.com/2001/01/22/technology/22COMP.html (accessed March 21, 2001).

169. NUA Internet Surveys, at www.nua.com (accessed October 3, 2000).

170. "Internet Access in America: Who's Got It, Who Needs It?" *CyberAtlas: The Web Marketers Guide to Online Facts* at cyberatlas.internet.com/big_picture/geographics/article/0,,5911_474291,00.html (accessed March 15, 2001).

171. National Telecommunications and Information Administration, *Falling through the Net: Toward Digital Inclusion.*

172. "Losing Ground Bit by Bit," *The Benton Foundation.*

173. "Losing Ground Bit by Bit," *The Benton Foundation.*

174. National Association of Community Action Agencies, "Information Technology for Community Action Agencies and Their Low-Income Clients" (Washington, D.C.: Summer 2000).

175. National Association of Community Action Agencies, "Information Technology for Community Action Agencies and Their Low-Income Clients."

176. Mark Simon, "Closing Our Digital Divide," *The San Francisco Chronicle*, March 23, 2000.

177. Henry Louis Gates, Jr., Opinion, *The New York Times*, October 31, 2000.

178. National Telecommunications and Information Administration, *Falling through the Net: Toward Digital Inclusion.*

179. National Telecommunications and Information Administration, *Falling through the Net: Toward Digital Inclusion.*

180. "Chinese Americans Have High PC and Internet Penetration Rates," *CyberAtlas: The Web Marketers Guide to Online Facts*, at cyberatlas.internet.com/big_picture/demographics/article/0,,5901_579671,00.html (accessed March 8, 2001).

181. "Chinese Americans Have High PC, and Internet Penetration Rates," *CyberAtlas.*

182. Garcia, "Researching Foundations on Successful Participation of Underrepresented Minorities in Information Technology."

183. National Telecommunications and Information Administration, *Falling through the Net: Toward Digital Inclusion.*

184. National Telecommunications and Information Administration, *Falling through the Net: Toward Digital Inclusion.*

185. National Telecommunications and Information Administration, *Falling through the Net: Toward Digital Inclusion.*

186. Pew Internet Project, "African Americans and the Internet" (Washington, D.C.: October 2000).

187. National School Boards Foundation, "Safe & Smart: Research and Guidelines for Children's Use of the Internet" (Washington, D.C.: March 2000).

188. National School Boards Foundation, "Safe & Smart."

189. National Telecommunications and Information Administration, *Falling through the Net.*

190. Gregory L. Rohde, Assistant Secretary for Communications and Information, National Telecommunications and Information Administration, U.S. Department of Commerce (testimony before U.S. Senate Committee on Agriculture, Nutrition, and Forestry, Washington, D.C.: February 3, 2000).

191. National Telecommunications and Information Administration, *Falling through the Net.*

192. National Telecommunications and Information Administration, *Falling through the Net.*

193. Rohde, National Telecommunications and Information Administration.

194. Pew Internet Project, "African Americans and the Internet."

195. Carrie Johnson, "Data Basics," *The Washington Post*, October 26, 2000.

196. Pew Internet Project, "African Americans and the Internet."

197. National Telecommunications and Information Administration, *Falling through the Net.*

198. National Telecommunications and Information Administration, *Falling through the Net.*

199. National Telecommunications and Information Administration, *Falling through the Net.*

200. National Telecommunications and Information Administration, *Falling through the Net.*

201. National Telecommunications and Information Administration, *Falling through the Net.*

202. National Telecommunications and Information Administration, *Falling through the Net.*

203. National Telecommunications and Information Administration, *Falling through the Net.*

204. National Telecommunications and Information Administration, *Falling through the Net.*

205. "Native Networking: Telecommunications and Information Technology in Indian Country," *The Benton Foundation* at www.digitaldividenetwork.org/content/sections/index.cfm?key=5 (accessed March 1, 2001).

206. "Native Networking: Telecommunications and Information Technology in Indian Country," *The Benton Foundation.*

207. "Native Networking: Telecommunications and Information Technology in Indian Country," *The Benton Foundation.*

208. "Native Networking: Telecommunications and Information Technology in Indian Country," *The Benton Foundation.*

209. "Native Networking: Telecommunications and Information Technology in Indian Country," *The Benton Foundation.*

210. Kade Twist, "Four Directions to Making the Internet Indian," *The Benton Foundation* at www.digitaldividenetwork.org/content/sections/index.cfm?key=4 (accessed March 1, 2001).

211. "Native Networking: Telecommunications and Information Technology in Indian Country," *The Benton Foundation.*

212. Charles Babington, "Phone Rates Will Rise to Expand Service for Indians," *The Washington Post*, at www.washingtonpost.com/ac2/wp-dyn?pagename=article&node=digest&contentId=A26337-2000Apr16 (accessed March 15, 2001).

213. Charles Babington, "Phone Rates Will Rise to Expand Service for Indians."

214. National Telecommunications and Information Administration, *Falling through the Net.*

215. National Telecommunications and Information Administration, *Falling through the Net.*

216. National Telecommunications and Information Administration, *Falling through the Net.*

217. National Telecommunications and Information Administration, *Falling through the Net.*

218. National Telecommunications and Information Administration, *Falling through the Net.*

219. Pew Internet Project, "Who's Not Online" (Washington, D.C.: September 2000).

220. The Southern Growth Policy Board, "Creating a CyberSouth."

221. David Plotnikoff, "Net Makes Rural Americans Less Isolated," *siliconvalley.com*, October 29, 2000.

222. Plotnikoff, "Net Makes Rural Americans Less Isolated," *siliconvalley.com.*

223. Plotnikoff, "Net Makes Rural Americans Less Isolated," *siliconvalley.com.*

224. Plotnikoff, "Net Makes Rural Americans Less Isolated," *siliconvalley.com.*

225. Plotnikoff, "Net Makes Rural Americans Less Isolated," *siliconvalley.com.*

226. Plotnikoff, "Net Makes Rural Americans Less Isolated," *siliconvalley.com.*

227. Plotnikoff, "Net Makes Rural Americans Less Isolated," *siliconvalley.com.*

228. Federal Communications Commission, "Federal Communications Commission Report on Deployment of High-Speed Internet."

229. National Telecommunications and Information Administration, US Department of Commerce, *Falling through the Net.*

230. General Accounting Office, "Characteristics and Choices of Internet Users."

231. Jill Lawrence, "Internet Inequality in Town and Country," *USA Today*, June 7, 2000.

232. Lawrence, "Internet Inequality in Town and Country."

232. Lawrence, "Internet Inequality in Town and Country."

233. Lawrence, "Internet Inequality in Town and Country."

234. Chris O'Malley, "The Digital Divide: Small Towns that Lack High-Speed Internet Access Find It Harder to Attract New Jobs," *Time Magazine* (March 22, 1999).

235. O'Malley, "The Digital Divide."

236. Parker, "Closing the Digital Divide in Rural America."

237. General Accounting Office, "Characteristics and Choices of Internet Users."

238. NUA Internet Surveys, "Senior Citizens Embrace the Web" at www.nua.ie/surveys/index.cgi?f=VS&art_id=905356057&rel=true (accessed April 5, 2001).

239. NUA Internet Surveys, at www.nua.ie/surveys/index.cgi?f=VS&art _id=905356066&rel=true (accessed April 5, 2001).

240. Pew Internet Project, "Who's Not Online?"

241. Pew Internet Project, "Who's Not Online?"

242. Pew Internet Project, "Who's Not Online?"

243. National Telecommunications and Information Administration, *Falling through the Net.*

244. Pew Internet Project, "Who's Not Online?"

245. Pew Internet Project, "Who's Not Online?"

246. Pew Internet Project, "Internet Tracking Report" (Washington, D.C.: February 2001).

247. Pew Internet Project, "Who's Not Online?"

248. Pew Internet Project, "Who's Not Online?"

249. UCLA Center for Communication Policy, "The UCLA Internet Report."

250. Jennifer LeClaire, "Widening Technology Gap Leaves Older Consumers by the Internet Wayside," *office.com*, winter 2000.

251. LeClaire, "Widening Technology Gap Leaves Older Consumers by the Internet Wayside."

252. LeClaire, "Widening Technology Gap Leaves Older Consumers by the Internet Wayside."

253. LeClaire, "Widening Technology Gap Leaves Older Consumers by the Internet Wayside."

254. Lisa LaNell Maudlin and Kelly Ford, "Digital Divide Initiatives: Are They Accessible to People with Disabilities?" at www.digitaldividenetwork .org/content/stories/index.cfm?key=76 (accessed March 1, 2001).

255. H. S. Kaye, "Disability Statistics Report (13): Computer and Internet Use Among People with Disabilities," National Institute on Disability and Rehabilitation Research (Washington, D.C.: U.S. Dept. of Education, 2000).

256. "Harkin Introduces Bill to Close Digital Divide for People with Disabilities" at harkin.senate.gov/~harkin/releases/00/10/2000A16945.html (accessed March 21, 2001).

257. Kaye, "Disability Statistics Report (13)."

258. Kaye, "Disability Statistics Report (13)."

259. Kaye, "Disability Statistics Report (13)."

260. National Telecommunications and Information Administration, *Falling through the Net.*

261. National Telecommunications and Information Administration, *Falling through the Net.*

262. Maudlin and Ford, "Digital Divide Initiatives."

263. Maudlin and Ford, "Digital Divide Initiatives."

264. Forrester Research, "The Web Accessibility Timebomb."

265. William E. Kennard, "Building Curb Cuts on the Information Highway" (speech before the National Association of the Deaf, July 3, 2000) at www.fcc.gov/Speeches/Kennard/2000/spwek016.html.

266. Adam Clayton Powell III, "U.S. Government Web Site Regulations Being Released Today," *The World Center*, March 12, 1999.

267. Powell, "U.S. Government Web Site Regulations Being Released Today."

268. PL 105-220, Workforce Investment Act Of 1998, Section 508–Electronic and Information Technology.

269. Powell, "U.S. Government Web Site Regulations Being Released Today."

270. Powell, "U.S. Government Web Site Regulations Being Released Today"

271. Alec Klein and Carrie Johnson, "Women Surf Past Men on Net," *The Washington Post* at www.washingtonpost.com/ac2/wp-dyn?pagename=article&node=digest&contentId=A137-2000Aug9 (accessed March 1, 2001).

272. National Telecommunications and Information Administration, *Falling through the Net.*

273. National Telecommunications and Information Administration, *Falling through the Net.*

274. National Telecommunications and Information Administration, *Falling through the Net.*

275. National Telecommunications and Information Administration, *Falling through the Net.*

276. National Telecommunications and Information Administration, *Falling through the Net.*

277. National Telecommunications and Information Administration, *Falling through the Net.*

278. National Telecommunications and Information Administration, *Falling through the Net.*

279. National Telecommunications and Information Administration, *Falling through the Net.*

280. National Telecommunications and Information Administration, *Falling through the Net.*

281. Pew Internet Project, "Who's Not Online?"

282. American Association of University Women Educational Foundation Research, "Tech-Savvy."

283. Twist, "Disparities along the Information Age Career Path," *The Benton Foundation*.

284. Carver, "Research Foundations for Improving the Representations of Women in the Information Technology Workforce."

285. American Association of University Women Educational Foundation Research, "Tech-Savvy."

286. Twist, "Disparities along the Information Age Career Path," *The Benton Foundation*.

287. American Association of University Women Educational Foundation Research, "Tech-Savvy."

CHAPTER 2

The Urgency of the Digital Divide

The [online] revolution has the strong potential to effect, in a very short time, structural, economic and social changes comparable to the Industrial Revolution.

—Japanese Prime Minister Yoshiro Mori[1]

The computer and the Internet give us the chance to move more people out of poverty more quickly than at any time in all of human history.

—President Bill Clinton[2]

Summary:

With the relevancy of the digital divide established, this chapter analyzes why it is a pressing, critical public policy issue by:

- Examining the social, economic, and political advances made by society's "underclasses" during other technological revolutions in history as a comparison, showing that in today's digital revolution there is a closing window of opportunity for social and economic betterment for today's disadvantaged groups.
- Demonstrating how the digital divide is a direct threat to the core principles of American democracy.
- Explaining how the digital divide poses an immediate and long-term danger to the health of America's economy.

Varying aspects of the digital divide were addressed in the first chapter. Despite the contrary opinions on the causes and scope of the digital divide, it is difficult to argue that the digital divide does not exist and does not pose a potentially vast social and economic problem. The purpose of this chapter is to answer the question: Why is the digital divide an urgent problem?

The urgency of the digital divide problem will be demonstrated in three ways. First, parallels between today's "Internet revolution" and past technological revolutions will be examined to show that there is a closing window of opportunity for social and economic parity.

Second, it will be shown that the technology haves and have-nots are diverging and that today's information-poor will be tomorrow's information-impoverished.[3]

Third, it will be shown that the future of America's economic development and the soundness of its democracy are at stake.

TECHNOLOGICAL REVOLUTIONS AND THE DISADVANTAGED

As Japanese Prime Minister Mori stated in the quote that began this chapter, the closest historical parallel to the current "digital revolution" in information technology is the Industrial Revolution of the nineteenth century. The Industrial Revolution was truly something like a cosmic explosion; it catapulted us from a rural and relatively stable past into the modern world we live in today. What made the Industrial Revolution possible was the capture of vast quantities of energy. Through new technology like the steam engine, power could be applied in a predictable and consistent way to the manufacture of goods and materials. Such goods could be produced in vast numbers to huge and expanding markets, changing forever the way people worked and lived.

The Industrial Revolution wrought enormous changes in the social fabric, creating modern capitalist economics and new patterns of wealth distribution. It led to the creation of the West as a distinct set of nations that enjoyed an overwhelming economic advantage over the rest of the world. The Third World was created by the new trading system of mercantilism that depended on taking raw materials from former colonies and then turning them back as finished goods for sale in a world market that now included them.[4]

Whereas the first phase of the Industrial Revolution, from about 1760 to 1829, was essentially the mechanized production of preexisting goods, the second phase, which came about with the introduction of the railway engine, enabled world markets to be opened up. This led to an unprecedented economic boom in Europe and the United States. This boom led to a shift in the balance of industrial and manufacturing power away from the traditional world leader, the United Kingdom, to the new economic powerhouse, the United States (table 2.1).

Table 2.1. Percentage of World's Manufacturing Production

	1870	1913
USA	23.3	35.8
Germany	13.2	15.7
UK	31.8	14.0
France	10.3	6.4
Russia	3.7	5.5

If the first phase of the Industrial Revolution was achieved by shortening the time it took to complete the production of goods, the second phase was accomplished by minimizing distance to markets.

Looking back to the Industrial Revolution in an effort to assess how far the current digital revolution has come reveals some interesting comparisons.

The advent of the computer can be compared to the first phase of the Industrial Revolution. Computing power drastically shortened the time and effort needed to complete the production of goods and services. For example, the blueprints for a building that would have taken months to draft by hand could be completed in days with the use of computers. The development of the Internet and the subsequent growth of e-commerce are analogous to the second phase of the Industrial Revolution. Both the Internet and e-commerce slash the distance between markets. With a mouse click, consumers are instantaneously connected to businesses. We are still at the very beginning stages of the second phase of the digital revolution, and we have a long way to go before we can say that the Internet has remade our world as the railway remade the world of the nineteenth century. Because the digital revolution's second phase is still in its infancy, however, there remains the opportunity to apply the lessons of the Industrial Revolution.

Beyond the advances in technology and commerce, one of the most significant contributions of the Industrial Revolution was the redistribution of wealth and the rise of the middle class. New industries and new markets provided the opportunity for ordinary people to accumulate relative wealth. Much like today, wealth in the nineteenth century brought better access to education and political power. As more people gained this access, a large middle class rose in society. People, who a generation before were rural, ill educated, and mostly disenfranchised, were now professional, educated, and politically active.

The transformations caused by the Industrial Revolution allowed previously disadvantaged people to "leap forward" and achieve social and economic advancement. Now, as the digital revolution blossoms in the early twenty-first century, there is the same opportunity for advancement.

The growth of e-commerce (the second phase of the digital revolution) has increased the demand for workers with Internet-related and information technology (IT) skills.[5]

- Between 1994 and 1998, IT jobs grew more than five times faster than all other occupations.[6]
- For example, software and computer services jobs doubled to more than 1.6 million.[7]

IT employment prospects look very favorable:

- The Bureau of Labor Statistics projects that 2 million new IT jobs will be created in the next ten years.[8]
- Higher-skilled IT jobs like computer engineers and system analysts are expected to grow from 874,000 in 1996 to 1.8 million in 2006.[9]
- The demand for programmers, database administrators, and network technicians is projected to grow 118 percent through 2006.[10]

Like the Industrial Revolution before it, the digital revolution has created a huge demand for new workers. And, as in the Industrial Revolution, these new jobs have the potential to create new wealth for those workers.

- In 1999, the average annual salary for an IT worker was $58,000, which is 85 percent higher than the national average of $31,400.[11]
- Computer engineers earn an average salary of approximately $60,000 a year and Web designers make an average of $53,000 a year.[12]
- Since 1992, salaries for IT workers have risen 5.8 percent annually, compared to only a 3.8 percent increase for other all other workers.[13]

Following the historical example of the Industrial Revolution, this new personal wealth will provide IT workers with greater access to education and political power.

Thus, there is a great possibility for the disadvantaged of today to make that same "leap forward" the emerging middle class did in the Industrial Revolution. In essence, there is the potential for the very people who are on the wrong side of the current digital divide to vault ahead economically and socially.

The key lies in access to the proper IT training for those who could benefit the most from the potential "leap forward": minorities, women, and the poor. With access to IT training, minorities, women, and the poor could take advantage of the current and future boom in IT jobs. Because IT jobs have higher average salaries and those salaries rise at close to twice the average rate, minorities, women, and the poor could quickly catch up in income to the rest of society. And as their income level rises, so will their political clout.

All of which hinges on the access to IT training. Without the access to training, the opportunity for advancement offered to the disadvantaged by the digital revolution is wasted. Clearly, more effort and emphasis needs to be placed to offer meaningful IT training to those groups who can benefit the most from it.

- Although African Americans constitute 10 percent of America's workforce, they only hold 5 percent of the economy's IT jobs.[14]

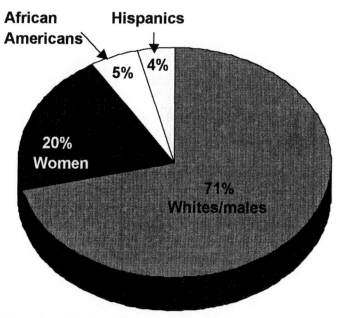

Figure 2.1. *Who holds IT jobs.*

- Although Hispanics make up 9 percent of America's workforce, they hold only 4 percent of the economy's IT jobs.[15]
- Women, half of America's workforce, hold only 20 percent of the economy's IT jobs.[16]
- Women earn only 15 percent of bachelor's degrees, 25.5 percent of master's degrees, and 12 percent of information technology-related doctoral degrees.[17]
- Women only earn approximately 27 percent of the bachelor's and master's degrees and 15 percent of computer science doctoral degrees;[18] computer science is the only academic field in which women's participation has actually decreased over time.[19]
- Moreover, there are disproportionately fewer women in both the IT education and training pipelines: only 17 percent of test takers in high school computer science advanced placement courses are female, and less than 10 percent are female in the higher-level computer science courses.[20]
- African Americans account for approximately 12 percent of the U.S. population, yet earn 11.17 percent of the bachelor's degrees, 5.38 percent of the master's degrees, and 1.78 percent of the doctoral degrees in computer science.[21]
- In the years 1990 to 1997, sixty-six African Americans earned Ph.D. degrees in computer science, translating to an average of only 9.4 per year.[22]
- Hispanics account for approximately 10.4 percent of the U.S. population, yet earn 5.84 percent of the bachelor's degrees, 3.07 percent of the master's degrees, and 0.97 percent of the doctoral degrees in computer science.[23]
- In the years 1990 to 1997, a total of 123 Hispanics earned Ph.D. degrees in computer science, translating to an average of 17.6 per year.[24]
- Native Americans account for approximately 0.7 percent of the U.S. population, yet earn 0.49 percent of the bachelor's degrees, 0.25 percent of the master's degrees, and 0.00 percent of the doctoral degrees in computer science.[25]
- In the years 1990 to 1997, a total of six Native Americans earned Ph.D. degrees in computer science, translating to an average of less than one per year.[26]

If women, minorities, and the poor do not receive better access to IT training today, then not only will they miss a historic opportunity, so will society as a whole.

TECHNOLOGY HAVES AND HAVE-NOTS:
CONVERGING OR DIVERGING?

Advances in computing technologies and market pressures have driven
the price of personal computers, which only a couple of years ago sold
for thousands of dollars, down to a few hundred dollars. In addition, if
a user is willing to tolerate extra advertisements, there are now free Internet services.[27] This, coupled with encouraging statistics on Internet
usage like the estimate that Internet traffic doubles every 100 days,[28]
leads many to assume that the digital divide is closing and that the technology haves and have-nots are converging. However, a closer examination of the realities of the Internet reveals that this is an overly opti-
mistic view. Thus, the second major reason why the digital divide is an
urgent problem is the fact that the technology haves and have-nots are
actually diverging.

Adoption and Diffusion

The Internet is often spoken of in the same terms of adoption and diffusion as other technologies. Adoption refers to the stage in which a
technology is selected for use by an individual or group, while diffusion is the stage in which the technology spreads to general use and application.[29] The adoption/diffusion model has been used to illustrate the
growth of everything from electricity to cell phones to the Internet. The
traditional adoption/diffusion continuum recognizes five categories of
new technology participants:

1. *Innovators* tend to be experimentalists and are often interested in
   new technology for the sake of technology.
2. *Early adopters* are technically sophisticated and are interested in
   technology for solving professional and academic problems.
3. *Early majority* are pragmatists and constitute the first part of the
   mainstream.
4. *Late majority* are not as comfortable with technology and are the
   skeptical second half of the mainstream.
5. *Laggards* may never adopt technology and may be critical and
   antagonistic of its use by others.[30]

If the Internet were a new technology like, say, television was fifty
years ago, it would be easy to claim that it has diffused through society
very quickly and that any real problem exists only for the remaining

laggards. However, this claim is faulty for two major reasons. First, the amazing speed of the Internet's adoption by some actually hinders its diffusion to all. Second, it ignores the fact that by its very nature the Internet is *not* comparable to other technologies like televisions or telephones.

Pace of Internet Adoption

There is little doubt about the remarkable pace of Internet adoption. If the point of when the Internet was available to the general public is usually agreed upon as 1993,[31] then the pace of Internet adoption eclipses all other technologies that have preceded it.[32] The typical technology adoption cycle is twenty years,[33] yet the Internet has proved to be a very precocious and atypical technology. For example, to reach the benchmark of fifty million users, it took radio thirty-eight years and television thirteen years; it only took fours years for the Internet to do so.[34] Looking at it another way, to reach one-third of American homes, electricity took fifty years, the telephone forty years, and television seventeen years—but the Internet spread to one-third of American households in just seven years.[35]

One of the major factors in the Internet's accelerated adoption is the "sustained explosion of [computer] microchip complexity—doubling year after year, decade after decade."[36] Remarkably, computer technology has obeyed "Moore's Law" (computing power will double every eighteen months) for over fifty years.[37] As computing horsepower has multiplied, not only has the Internet been made possible, it has been made accessible and usable to most ordinary people. In 1946, the

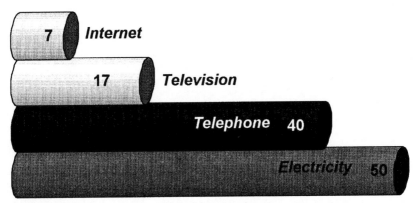

Figure 2.2.   *Years to reach one-third of American homes.*

world's first programmable computer, ENIAC, was 150 feet wide, cost millions of dollars, and could execute 5,000 operations per second.[38] Twenty-five years later, twelve times ENIAC's processing power could fit into a postage stamp-sized chip that cost $200.[39] Today, an average personal computer can perform over 400 million instructions per second (MIPS).[40] In the last six years, the cost of microprocessor computing power has decreased from $230 per MIPS to $3.42 per MIPS.[41] No other manufactured item has fallen in price so far, so fast.[42]

All this being said, one would assume that the digital divide would be closing at a brisk pace. It is a fact that the Internet, fueled by ever more powerful and affordable computing technology, has been adopted by over 100 million Americans, up from 1.3 million in 1993.[43] But this begs the question: what about the other 170 million or so Americans who have not yet adopted the Internet? Are they the "late majority" in the adoption/diffusion model? So, maybe, it is not an issue of technology haves and have-nots but of "have-nows" and "have-laters"?[44] Unfortunately, this is not the case. Instead of converging, the technology haves and have-nots are actually diverging.

This divergence is caused by two major factors. First, involuntary barriers impede Internet adoption by certain groups. Second, due to the startling pace of technology's evolution, late adopters may never catch up to the early adopters and the early majority.

Involuntary Barriers to Adoption

Although falling computer prices have been trumpeted as the swan song for the digital divide, the high price of technology is still a major involuntary barrier for many potential users. Recent studies by the Pew Internet Project and the Kaiser Family Foundation bear this point out: 39 percent of people not online say the reason they do not access the Internet is because it is too expensive;[45] and for those who do not have a computer at home, 33 percent said the reason is computers are too expensive.[46]

Although computer prices have fallen, the cost of the technology must be looked at in relative terms. Yes, if you are making $50,000 a year then a $500 computer and $19.95 a month Internet access are economically feasible. But what about the 32.3 million poor Americans whose annual income for a family of four is $17,029[47]—can they justify the expense of even the most basic computer? For the poor, the added cost of a computer and Internet access (not even including additional costs like software, training, increased utility charges, etc.) would not only be a financial burden, it might be financially crippling.

Though the relatively high price of technology is still a large involuntary barrier to Internet adoption, even if computers were free and broadband connections widely available, there would remain usability barriers.[48] Of Americans not currently online, 36 percent said the reason is the Internet is "too confusing."[49]

The HomeNet field trial conducted by Carnegie Mellon University best demonstrates the usability problems of the Internet.[50] In this study, families were provided a Macintosh computer with a modem connected to a dedicated phone line. The computers were outfitted with a turnkey system for Internet access meaning that the software was configured so that family members did not need to learn any details of the computer's operating system to access the Internet. In addition, each family received nearly three hours of computer and Internet training. With all this in place, over 70 percent of the families still called the trial's help desk with problems using their computers and the Internet. The study concluded that "computer skill still predicted Internet usage significantly. . . . This result held true across different gender and age groups. . . . Participants who reported difficulty tended not to use the Internet much."

Even for a seasoned user, computers and the Internet can still be tricky or outright difficult to use. Do you know how to disable cookies on your Internet browser? Know how to add the POP and SMTP servers of a new account to your e-mail program? Ever get a baffling error message for no apparent reason? Now imagine trying to find the proper link on a black-on-purple Web page if you have poor vision, or trying to follow a dense computer manual if English is not your primary language. The design of computers and the Internet needs to be substantially improved to enable usage by all people,[51] especially people faced with the involuntary barriers of language and educational limitations or physical disabilities.

Risks of Late Adoption

Is there a problem if, due to either voluntary choice or involuntary barriers, a person does not adopt Internet technology until late? After all, as long as everyone *eventually* gains access, then everyone will have access . . . but the problem is that late adopters might not have *equal* access.

It is important to note who in American society is at direct risk due to late adoption. In its 2000 study "Who's Not Online?" the Pew Internet Project analyzed the demographics of non-Internet users.[52] The findings of this study revealed some disquieting patterns in those who are "reluctant" to use the Internet (corresponding to the *late majority* in the adoption/diffusion model) and who will "never" use the Internet (the *laggards* in the adoption/diffusion model).

For the "Reluctants":

- 56 percent are female.
- 64 percent are over the age of fifty.
- 76 percent have a high school degree or less.
- 65 percent live in households earning $50,000 or less.

For the "Nevers":

- 57 percent are female.
- 81 percent are over the age of fifty.
- 82 percent have a high school diploma or less.
- 43 percent earn $30,000 or less.

Most tellingly, age and education level are the two most significant characteristics of the late majority and the laggards. This is critical because the Internet is "evolving upwards"—it is becoming exponentially more complex every day.[53] A few years ago, the primary use of the Internet was e-mail. Today, the Internet is used for everything from securing a mortgage and filing taxes to taking courses for college credit and finding a new career. Even the mainstay of e-mail has evolved from simple text to video and audio messages. All of this new complexity requires skills and knowledge earned through hands-on experience.

According to UCLA's "Surveying the Digital Future" report, the most experienced Internet users (more than four years of Internet experience) use the Internet 2.5 times as much (16.2 hours a week) as those with less than a year of Internet experience (6.1 hours a week).[54] Moreover, the most experienced Internet users spend a greater amount of time online working from home, reading news, and making investments, while the least experienced Internet users spend more time playing online games and pursuing hobbies. Thus, late adopters face the risk of being unable to optimize their eventual access to the Internet due to their lack of experience. It is analogous to expecting a person who just got their driver's license to drive a tractor-trailer with a twelve-speed manual transmission on a busy highway. Yes, late adopters will have access, but they will not have equal access if they lack the experience and "information literacy"[55] to use their access effectively.

Another risk late adopters face is being shut out from the current wealth of information and opportunities available via the Internet. Take, for example, the fact that 93 percent of federal, state, and local government agencies or divisions maintain a public website.[56] Eighty-three percent of these websites allow citizens to view and download government documents, 73 percent post legislative and regulatory bodies' calendars of proceedings, and 64 percent have feedback/comment mechanisms.[57] Moreover, 90 percent of local government websites will soon allow citizens pay tickets/fines, utility bills, and taxes.[58]

Speaking of taxes, late adopters are missing out on the opportunity and thus the benefits of filing their federal taxes online. The benefits of online filing are twofold. First, returns on online filings are processed much more rapidly: twenty-one days on average for online returns compared to forty days for paper returns.[59] Second, the error rate for online filings is less than 1 percent, compared to a 16 percent error rate for paper returns.[60]

Another example of vital government information and services available online that late adopters are missing out on is the location and toxicity of hazardous waste sites near their homes.[61] As background, one in five Americans lives within four miles of one of the 1,400 hazardous waste sites seriously contaminated enough to make the EPA's Superfund's National Priorities List (NPL).[62] In addition, there are nearly 9,000 other Superfund hazardous waste sites not listed on the NPL.[63] The location and toxicity of these sites is easily available to a homeowner (or a homebuyer) on websites like e-risk.com or nearmyhome.com.[64] But for those not online, this information is buried in dense, paper volumes located in a government building in Washington, D.C.[65]

As "government bodies, community organizations, and corporations are displacing resources from their ordinary channels of communications onto the Internet,"[66] the longer late adopters delay (or are delayed), the more they are denied information. In other words, as the Internet becomes *the* source and medium of information, late adopters are at risk of not just becoming "information poor" but "information impoverished."[67]

The Internet Is Not Analogous to Other Technologies

Although the Internet has far outpaced the adoption rate of other technologies, parallels are often drawn between the Internet and preceding technologies. Because of the skewed perception that the Internet is only a communication and entertainment tool, analogies between the Internet and the telephone and television are the most convenient to make. By wedding the facts of the Internet's rapid adoption rate with the easy analogies of the Internet and the telephone and television, many claim that the digital divide will soon close as Internet technologies diffuse throughout society. For example: "Once . . . televisions were a rare and expensive device that only a few households were lucky enough to possess, and now every home has nearly one TV per person. . . . [Like the Internet,] most advanced technologies that are available only to an elite few become widely dispersed among the broader population." [68]

Yet arguments based on Internet and telephone/television analogies are shaky at best because they ignore the basic fact that the Internet is fundamentally different from any other technology. Thus, any analogies drawn between the Internet and other technologies are meaningless because comparing the Internet to the telephone or television is just like comparing apples to oranges.

There are three major ways that the Internet differs from other technologies. First, the Internet has a much more complex set of prerequisites for usage. Second, the Internet offers higher rewards to more expert users. And third, the speed of innovation in Internet technology means that the technology is constantly evolving and reinventing itself, unlike the relatively static technology of the telephone and television.

First, before the Internet can be used effectively, it is necessary for a complicated and interconnected set of prerequisites to be in place. In broad strokes, this includes access to an Internet-ready computer; the knowledge of how to use the computer and its modem to connect to the Internet; how to navigate within the Internet; how to use the Internet browser and e-mail programs' software; how to save information gleaned from the Internet, and so forth. Each of these points is built upon even more prerequisites like the ability to type, having touch-tone phone service, a credit card to charge Internet purchases, knowledge of Boolean searches, etc. And the prerequisites for telephone service? A telephone line, a telephone, and the abilities to dial, speak, and listen. The prerequisites for television are even simpler: electricity to operate the set and the ability to turn it on and off. Television is a very passive form of entertainment technology in which users just sit back and watch. The Internet, however, is a dynamic information technology that requires the "active, informed, literate participation of the user." [69]

Second, unlike the telephone and television, the Internet offers higher rewards for expert users. The more Internet skills a user has, the greater benefits from the Internet the user will gain. Take, for example, the common practice of using the Internet for research. Say, three people of varying Internet abilities want to research the topic of the digital divide. A novice Internet user might go to a popular search engine, type in *digital divide*, then wade through the mountain of Web pages that contain the words *digital* and/or *divide* until they eventually find something relevant. A more skilled user might use a Boolean search like *"digital divide"* + *"statistics"* to produce a short list of Web pages with statistics about the digital divide. An advanced user might use an automated, programmable "bot" to scour the Internet for specific information about the digital divide while the user is offline and then have the information distilled into a concise summary that is e-mailed to him or her. The expert user therefore gains the greatest benefit. Because telephones and televisions are such relatively one-dimensional technologies, all users, whether they have been exposed to the technology for a day or fifteen years, receive the same rewards from the technology.

Third, constant innovations mean that the Internet is perpetually changing in scope and applications. In the few years of the Internet's existence, it has evolved from a text-only messaging "bulletin board" to a dynamic, multimedia bazaar with streaming audio and full-motion video. With the advent of broadband connections and personal computers with greater microprocessor power than NASA's Apollo project, what was once thought impractical or even impossible is now commonplace on the Internet. As the Internet moves into everything from cell phones to gas pumps, who can accurately predict what the Internet's capabilities will be in the future?

In contrast, telephone technology, with the exception of touch-tone service, has remained basically unchanged since Bell first summoned Watson. The same holds true with the technology of television. Granted, television changed from black-and-white to color and is now toddling towards digital and telephones moved from crank-operated to cordless, but these were essentially refinements of the basic technologies, not reinventions of the technology like those on the Internet.

In summary, while it is difficult to dispute the pace of Internet adoption, it is wrong to assume that rapid adoption will result in equal diffusion to all. In terms of the digital divide, this means that relative inequality will increase even as Internet use spreads. As technology haves and have-nots diverge, the debate in the near future will be more about the technology "have-alls" and the "have-somes."

WHAT IS AT STAKE DOMESTICALLY?

The third reason why the digital divide is an urgent problem is that both the health of America's democracy and its future economic development are at stake.

To gain a better perspective on these issues, it is best to review how prior technology revolutions impacted democracy and economic growth. Earlier in this chapter, today's digital revolution was compared to the Industrial Revolution to show the opportunity for economic and political advancement for the disadvantaged. However, for the terms of discussing the issues of American democracy and economic progress, the historical parallel between the development of the Internet and the invention of the printing press is a more relevant and enlightening comparison. Granted, it is premature to claim that the Internet will be a history-shaping catalyst on the same epic scale of the printing press. However, by looking at both the Internet and the printing press as *information access tools*, the lessons learned from the printing press show that the Internet has the potential to strengthen America's democracy and economy. Conversely, if the digital divide in Internet access is allowed to remain or even widen, then the very future of our democracy and prosperity is at stake.

The printing press challenged the power of the old priesthood of a literate elite that maintained their power and influence by monopolizing access to the written word. Before Guttenberg invented the movable type printing press, ordinary people had access only to the information that the literate elite allowed them to have. With the printing press, access to information and ideas was liberated. Massive social and political change ensued—from the development of the Protestant Reformation to the founding of the modern university to the birth of democracy and nationalism.

Harkening back to similar arguments about adoption and diffusion, many see the Internet not as a tool for information access like the printing press, but as a communication device like radio or television. This ignores the fact that radio and television are both inventions that emerged within a society and culture with over a century of mass literacy. Therefore, the introduction of radio and television did not challenge a ruling literate elite as the printing press did. In fact, both television and radio followed the mass circulation newspaper in terms of increasing the power of a new elite—the media. Press barons of the early part of the twentieth century like William Randolph Hearst are not so different from the media conglomerations like AOL/Time Warner and Disney/ABC of this century.

Like the printing press, the Internet allows ordinary people to access information on their own terms. The difference that the Internet makes is that it offers a rapid, global, two-way communication channel. This enables a larger segment of the public more opportunities to not only shape how they receive their information but, for the first time in human history, facilitates the means for any individual to speak to virtually a worldwide audience. This ability to offer two-way communication for anyone who can type and can be connected to a modem is perhaps the most radical idea since the printing press. What then is at stake domestically is the redefinition of what it means to be a citizen in the new "wired" America.

This leaves open the probability that large numbers of people will be left behind as this huge technological wave takes the more affluent groups to a new level. Arguably, what is therefore at stake is the future of our democracy and our economy. If we make decisions that are either explicitly or have the net effect of disenfranchising large groups of people from the new democracy and economy that we are creating, then we would have some dire consequences to face in the very near future.

Issues of Democracy

There are two major implications of the digital divide for American democracy. First is how the digital divide affects the basic principles of democracy. Second is how the Internet is evolving into an alleged enabler of the democratic process.

At its core, democracy demands participation of its citizens. Full participation in a democracy requires universal access to knowledge and information.[70] As Thomas Jefferson said, "self-government depend[s] on the free, unhampered pursuit of truth by an informed and involved citizenry."[71] The Internet has made it possible for people to access information and communicate ideas with unparalleled ease and depth.[72] There is an incredible wealth and diversity of political resources available on the Internet related to the "task of creating morally responsible citizens."[73] For example, on the Internet, people can easily explore detailed positions of a candidate's platform, view the voting record of an incumbent, obtain a list of financial contributors to a political party, and communicate directly with government agencies.

The digital divide directly impacts the fundamental principle of political participation in American democracy. If a segment of the population does not have equal access to the Internet, they do not have equal access to the online political resources. Therefore, without access to the same information as the rest of society, those on the wrong side of the digital divide are denied equal political participation. Without universal, unhindered access to online information, American democracy is at risk of losing full participation by all of its citizens in the governing process.

The second area where the Internet is impacting American democracy is the prospect of online voting, or "e-voting." E-voting is already being experimented with as an alternative to traditional balloting methods. The states of Arizona, Florida, Iowa, Washington, and California are all exploring the possibility of e-voting.[74]

It is purported that e-voting will expand the democratic process by improving voter turnout by increasing access to the millions of eligible voters who do not regularly participate in the elections.[75] With fewer than half of eligible voters age twenty-four to thirty-four, and less than 40 percent of eligible eighteen- to twenty-year-olds registered to vote, it is hoped that e-voting will bring more younger voters into the democratic process.[76]

Furthermore, in light of the controversy and resulting circus of Florida's disputed paper ballots in the 2000 presidential election, many point to e-voting as a logical, evolutionary step in the democratic process. With simple, precise e-voting, there would have been no "hanging or pregnant chads" to begin with.

However, if e-voting gains wide acceptance, the digital divide could introduce unacceptable biases into the election, as those who would take advantage of the great convenience of voting at home via their personal computer would be primarily in the middle and upper classes.[77] This potential skewing of voter turnout would be inconsistent with basic democratic precepts, which mandate fairness and equal access in elections.[78]

Economic Issues

As previously mentioned, the digital revolution has had a huge impact on the economy.

- The Internet economy directly supports 3.088 million jobs— 60,000 more than the entire insurance industry and nearly double the number of people employed by the real estate industry.[79]

- The Internet economy generated an estimated $830 billion in revenues in 2000.[80]

This caused a massive demand for skilled information technology workers.

- The demand for higher-skilled IT workers like computer engineers and systems analysts will grow from 874,00 to 1.8 million in 2006.[81] These positions generally require a four-year undergraduate degree and, in many cases, advanced training or a graduate degree.[82]
- In contrast, lesser-skilled IT-related jobs like computer operators and duplication machine operators are expected to drop from 481,000 to 342,000 by 2006.[83]
- The need for the higher-skilled positions is growing even as the number of American college graduates with high-tech degrees is falling: 207,056 high-tech degrees were awarded in 1997, down 2 percent since 1990.[84]

Although demand for IT workers has fallen recently from 10.4 million to 9.9 million, there remains a shortage of 600,000 IT workers in 2002.[85] This lack of skilled IT workers is a real and immediate threat to America's present prosperity and continued economic stability. Chairman of the Federal Reserve Board Alan Greenspan warned that the U.S. economy can only remain robust if emerging "imbalances" like the shrinking pool of skilled IT workers are corrected.[86] To Chairman Greenspan, often regarded as the most influential voice in the economy, imbalances like the widening gap in supply and demand of skilled IT workers could undermine the economy: "Only a balanced prosperity can continue indefinitely. One that is [imbalanced] will eventually falter."[87]

Nations that have an insufficient supply of skilled IT workers will soon see highly skilled and high-paying IT jobs migrate to countries that can supply the needed talent.[88] Even though the United States has led the world in the digital revolution, without a concerted effort to train students and workers to meet the challenges of the digital economy, the United States could face a migration of high-skill, high-wage jobs to other countries.[89]

NOTES

1. "Why We Need to Close the Divide: Several Views on Why It Must Be Done," *ABC News.com* at www.abcnews.com (accessed July 22, 2000).

2. Edwin Chin, "Conferees Debate U.S. Prosperity," *Los Angeles Times*, April 6, 2000.

3. "Losing Ground Bit by Bit: Low-Income Communities in the Information Age," *The Benton Foundation* at www.digitaldividenetwork.org/content/sections/index.cfm?key=5 (accessed March 1, 2000).

4. Paul Hasall, "Modern History Sourcebook: Tables Illustrating the Spread of Industrialization," *Internet Modern History Sourcebook* at www.fordham.edu/halsall/mod/indrevtabs1.html (accessed March 23, 2001).

5. Economics and Statistics Administration, "Digital Economy 2000" (Washington, D.C.: U.S. Dept. of Commerce, 2000).

6. Economics and Statistics Administration, "Digital Economy 2000."

7. Economics and Statistics Administration, "Digital Economy 2000."

8. "U.S. Government Electronic Commerce Policy," *U.S. Department of Commerce* at www.ecommerce.gov/danc1.htm (accessed March 3, 2001).

9. "U.S. Government Electronic Commerce Policy," *U.S. Department of Commerce*.

10. Oscar N. Garcia, "Researching Foundations on Successful Participation of Underrepresented Minorities in Information Technology" (Wright University, November 1999).

11. Economics and Statistics Administration, "Digital Economy 2000."

12. Economics and Statistics Administration, "Digital Economy 2000."

13. Economics and Statistics Administration, "Digital Economy 2000."

14. John Simons, "Cheap Computers Bridge Digital Divide," *The Wall Street Journal*, January 27, 2000.

15. Simons, "Cheap Computers Bridge Digital Divide."

16. American Association of University Women Educational Foundation Research "Tech-Savvy: Educating Girls in the New Computer Age" (Washington, D.C.: AAUW, 2000).

17. Kade Twist, "Disparities along the Information Age Career Path," *The Benton Foundation* at www.digitaldividenetwork.org/content/sections/index.cfm?key=5 (accessed March 1, 2001).

18. Doris L. Carver, "Research Foundations for Improving the Representations of Women in the Information Technology Workforce" (Louisiana State University, November 1999).

19. American Association of University Women Educational Foundation Research, "Tech-Savvy."

20. American Association of University Women Educational Foundation Research, "Tech-Savvy."

21. Oscar N. Garcia, "Researching Foundations on Successful Participation of Underrepresented Minorities in Information Technology" (Wright University, November 1999).

22. Garcia, "Researching Foundations on Successful Participation of Underrepresented Minorities in Information Technology."

23. Garcia, "Researching Foundations on Successful Participation of Underrepresented Minorities in Information Technology."

24. Garcia, "Researching Foundations on Successful Participation of Underrepresented Minorities in Information Technology."

25. Garcia, "Researching Foundations on Successful Participation of Underrepresented Minorities in Information Technology."

26. Garcia, "Researching Foundations on Successful Participation of Underrepresented Minorities in Information Technology."

27. Jacob Sullum, "Gap Credibility," *Reason Magazine*, February 16, 2000.

28. "U.S. Government Electronic Commerce Policy," U.S. Department of Commerce.

29. V. H. Carr, Jr, "Technology Adoption and Diffusion," The Learning Center for Interactive Technology (Washington, D.C.: U.S. National Library of Medicine, 1998).

30. Carr, "Technology Adoption and Diffusion."

31. Stephen Rizzo, "Is There Really a Digital Divide in America?" *The O'Reilly Network*, June 7, 2000.

32. "U.S. Government Electronic Commerce Policy," *U.S. Department of Commerce*.

33. Harris N. Miller, "The ITAA Digital Opportunity Initiative" (remarks before the House Committee on Small Business, March 28, 2000).

34. "U.S. Government Electronic Commerce Policy," *U.S. Department of Commerce*.

35. Paul Van Slambrouck, "Internet Becomes the New Family Hearth," *The Christian Science Monitor*, October 26, 2000.

36. Michael Riordan and Lillian Hoddeson, *Crystal Fire: The Birth of the Information Age* (Boston, Mass.: Norton, 1997).

37. "U.S. Government Electronic Commerce Policy," *U.S. Department of Commerce*.

38. "U.S. Government Electronic Commerce Policy," *U.S. Department of Commerce*.

39. "U.S. Government Electronic Commerce Policy," *U.S. Department of Commerce*.

40. "U.S. Government Electronic Commerce Policy," *U.S. Department of Commerce*.

41. "U.S. Government Electronic Commerce Policy," *U.S. Department of Commerce*.

42. "U.S. Government Electronic Commerce Policy," *U.S. Department of Commerce*.

43. Miller, "The ITAA Digital Opportunity Initiative."

44. David Boaz "A Snapshot View of a Complex World," *IntellectualCapital .com* at www.intellectualcapital.com/issues/issue257/item5729.asp (accessed November 20, 2000).

45. Pew Internet Project, "Who's Not Online?" (Washington, D.C.: September 2000).

46. "National Public Radio/Kaiser Family Foundation/Kennedy School of Government Survey of Americans on Technology," February 2000.

47. Bureau of the Census, *1999 Income and Poverty Estimates* (Washington, D.C.: 1999.)

48. Ben Schneiderman (remarks before the Conference on Universal Usability, November 2000).

49. Pew Internet Project, "Who's Not Online?"

50. "Usability, Help Desk Calls, and Residential Internet Usage," Carnegie Mellon University.

51. Schneiderman (remarks).

52. Pew Internet Project, "Who's Not Online?"

53. Christy Mumford Jerding, "True Nature of 'Digital Divide' Divides Experts," *The Freedom Forum Online*, March 17, 2000.

54. UCLA Center for Communication Policy, "The UCLA Internet Report: Surveying the Digital Future" (Los Angeles: University of Southern California, November 2000).

55. Jerding, "True Nature of 'Digital Divide' Dives Experts."

56. Council for Excellence in Government, "E-Government: The Next American Revolution" at www.excelgov.org/egovpoll/index.htm (accessed March 1, 2001).

57. Council for Excellence in Government, "E-Government."

58. NUA Internet Surveys, "Majority of U.S. Local Governments Now Online" at www.nua.ie/surveys/index.cgi?f=VS&art_id=905356508&rel=true (accessed March 1, 2001).

59. Eileen Alt, "More and More Americans Filing Taxes Online," *Nando Times*, March 8, 2001.

60. Alt, "More and More Americans Filing Taxes Online."

61. Larry Tuttle, "The Digital Divide and Environmental Access," *Oregonlive.com* at www.oregonlive.com/oped/index.ssf?/oped/00/04/ed042455 .frame (accessed April 20, 2001).

62. Tuttle, "The Digital Divide and Environmental Access."

63. Tuttle, "The Digital Divide and Environmental Access."

64. Tuttle, "The Digital Divide and Environmental Access."

65. Tuttle, "The Digital Divide and Environmental Access."

66. "Losing Ground Bit by Bit: Low-Income Communities in the Information Age," *The Benton Foundation*.

67. "Losing Ground Bit by Bit: Low-Income Communities in the Information Age," *The Benton Foundation*.

68. Jacob Sullum, "Gap Credibility," *Reason Magazine*, February 16, 2000.

69. Don Tapscott, *Growing Up Digital* (New York: McGraw-Hill, 1997).

70. David M. Anderson, "The Digital Divide Conceals a Deeper Divide," *IntellectualCapital.com*, December 16, 1999.

71. Erin Marie Walsh, "Access to Information Technology in the Face of the Growing Digital Divide" at www.priceton.edu/~emwalsh/ (accessed March 2, 2001).

72 Walsh, "Access to Information Technology."

73. Anderson, "The Digital Divide Conceals a Deeper Divide."

74. Kevin Anderson, "Opening Up the Digital Democracy," *BBC News Online* at news.bbc.co.uk/hi/english/in_depth/americas/2000/us_elections/vote_usa_2000/newsid_597000/597304.stm (accessed January 10, 2000).

75. April Pederson, "Online Voting Puts Web to the Test," *Policy.com*, July 31, 2000.

76. Angelica Pence, "Cyberspace Voting Wins Approval," *San Francisco Chronicle*, November 7, 2000.

77. Pederson, "Online Voting Puts Web to the Test."

78. Pederson, "Online Voting Puts Web to the Test."

79. NUA Internet Surveys, "Internet Supports 3 Million U.S. Jobs" at www.nua.ie/surveys/index.cgi?f=VS&art_id=905356340&rel=true (accessed March 8, 2001).

80. NUA Internet Surveys, "Internet Supports 3 Million U.S. Jobs."

81. "U.S. Government Electronic Commerce Policy," *U.S. Department of Commerce*.

82. "U.S. Government Electronic Commerce Policy," *U.S. Department of Commerce*.

83. "U.S. Government Electronic Commerce Policy," *U.S. Department of Commerce*.

84. Marjorie Valbruin, "Groups Says Visas Widen Digital Divide," *The Wall Street Journal*, July 7, 2000.

85. "Study Sees IT Worker Shortage in 2002," *News.com* at www.news.com (accessed May 6, 2002).

86. "Testimony of Chairman Alan Greenspan before the Joint Economic Committee," U.S. Congress, June 17, 1999 (Washington, D.C.: Federal Reserve Board).

87. Chin, "Conferees Debate U.S. Prosperity," *Los Angeles Times.*

88. "U.S. Government Electronic Commerce Policy," *U.S. Department of Commerce*.

89. "U.S. Government Electronic Commerce Policy," *U.S. Department of Commerce*.

CHAPTER 3

The Digital Divide and Education

Advantage magnifies advantage. . . . While education is the great equalizer, technology appears to be a new engine of inequality.

—Lawrence Gladieux, The College Board[1]

If we can't put computers or the Internet in every home, what can we do? [Schools] spend $7 billion on technology each year, but only 16 [percent] to 18 percent of teachers feel comfortable using it. If one child fails in school due to lack of access, that's one child too many.

—Prof. Joyce Pittman, University of Cincinnati[2]

The real divide is in educational achievement, not just digital access.

—George W. Bush[3]

Summary:

This chapter explores the digital divide in America's education system. After establishing the importance of technology in learning, the disparities in technology access for high-poverty and high-minority schools is addressed along with the overall lack of technology training for the nation's teachers. Solutions to the education digital divide are presented by reviewing the federal government's efforts; offering local, regional, and nationwide strategies; and studying working programs that might serve as models for success.

With the reality and urgency of the digital divide established in the preceding chapters, this chapter focuses on the critical issue of the digital divide in education. This issue will be explored by:

- Showing how technology promotes learning, and
- Delineating the facts of the digital divide within the nation's schools and classrooms.

Then we will:

- Present the key challenges in the education digital divide.
- Discuss the efforts by the federal government.
- Offer workable solutions.

Furthermore, through four case studies, potential local, regional, and national models for addressing digital divide issues in education will be discussed.

DOES TECHNOLOGY PROMOTE LEARNING?

Before any discussion can take place about the digital divide in education, the relevancy of technology in the classroom must be addressed. After all, if computers and the Internet do not promote learning, any disparity in educational technology access is a moot point.

A recent report titled "Fool's Gold: A Critical Look at Computers in Childhood," authored by the Alliance for Childhood, calls for a nationwide halt to the introduction of computers in elementary classrooms and in early childhood programs—with the exception of computers to aid children with learning disabilities. Endorsed by eighty-two education experts, including Larry Cuban of Stanford University and Diane Ravitch, former Assistant Secretary of Education, the report should give the educational technology advocates pause. It comes at a time when others are questioning the escalating costs of educational technology and wondering out loud what difference it is making to student achievement.

Despite the voices to the contrary, computers and the Internet are vital learning tools necessary to prepare students for an ever-increasingly "wired" society and economy.

The use of technology in education can be traced back to the use of radio, television, and the film projector. A pattern of high expectations for the potential of these technologies followed by their marginalization has led many to believe that the same fate awaits computers. The difference with the application of computer technologies in the classroom is that computers have evolved and become more complex and useful with the passage of time, whereas the other inventions referenced have not fundamentally changed since their introduction.

A further distinction is that inventions like television and radio are one-way media and do not allow for interactivity and individualization—a key asset of computer technologies. If we look at the evolution of the computer, we see the emergence of at least four distinct adaptations of the technology to classroom teaching and learning:

- As a supplement or augmentation for the teacher through "computer assisted instruction" (CAI) to teach the traditional curriculum primarily on the teaching of basic skills. Following the introduction of the more user-friendly personal computer in the 1980s, teachers have used a variety of software to respond to individual student needs. In many cases, this has had a prime emphasis on reading and math in the early grades and remedial "drill and practice" formats for other users.
- As an aid to cognitive development. Here we can refer to the efforts during the 1980s to teach computer programming, using languages such as LOGO, Pascal, BASIC, and Cobol.
- As a creative tool to aid "constructivist learning." In contrast to students being seen as passively receiving information and practicing their skills within specified formats, students would create their own multimedia presentations, solve problems, and respond to simulations.
- As a tool to enable individualized distance learning to take place. Even though this has radically affected the nature of postsecondary education, its effects have yet to be felt in the realm of elementary and secondary education.

Most of the research we have about educational technology's effectiveness dates back to the days of "drill and practice" and computer aided instruction. The research suggests that certain types of software for narrowly prescribed purposes can raise student achievement test scores over time.[4] There is also evidence that technology can positively affect students' motivation to learn.[5]

It has been more difficult, however, to establish positive effects on students from more contemporary uses of the computer. This has been mainly due to weak methodologies and the lack of random-control experiments. Where the research exists, it shows that computers have positive effects for disadvantaged students. A study of West Virginia's Basic Skills-Computer Education program found a positive increase in test scores, especially among poor and low-income students.[6] An Educational Testing Service study found that those students working on problem solving rather than drill and practice registered the greatest gains.[7]

THE NATURE OF THE EDUCATION DIVIDE

What is the nature of the digital divide when it comes to education? If that question had been posed in the early 1990s, the answer would most probably be different than if the question were posed today.

Back in the early 1990s, the challenge was connecting schools to the Internet. The divide was clearly between those suburban schools that made aggressive efforts to wire their buildings (often with the help of parents who knew that their children's futures were intimately bound up with their ability to master technology) and the inner-city and rural schools that lacked funds and as much dedicated business support as their suburban counterparts to connect to the Web or the "information superhighway" as it was then being called.

But within the decade, as the most recent survey of Internet access reveals, over 90 percent of public schools in the United States were connected to the Internet, nearly reaching the goal of connecting every school; the number of schools connected soared from 35 percent in 1994 to 95 percent in 1999 (figure 3.1).

Ask about the nature of the digital divide today as we look at the issue from the early years of the twenty-first century, and we find the issue is disproportionate classroom access—most schools may be connected but not every classroom, and the numbers vary according to school poverty level. There is also the issue of student-to-computer ratio and teacher qualification, as well as speed of connectivity.

Although these issues were not forgotten in the prior decade, they were viewed as not as important as just getting schools connected to the Internet . . . even if it was only one instructional room or, worse still, just the principal's office. Our point is to show that despite the success we have experienced in connecting most schools to the Internet, "digital divide issues" are constantly shifting. As we make advances, and as the prices of various types of equipment, networking, or software de-

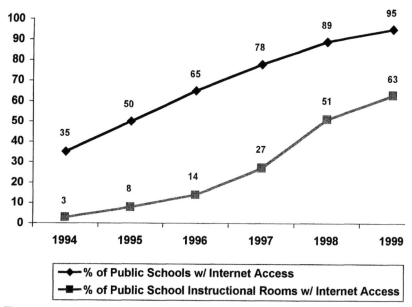

Figure 3.1. *Internet access in schools/instructional rooms.*

cline, a new set of equity and access issues arrives. This is the price of progress, some might say, just as the burdens of progress were never fairly shared. There have always been winners and losers with any new invention, from the steam engine to the car to electricity and the phone.

The educational digital divide happens when some of those on the losing edge of progress are children, poor, or minorities who want to gain a foothold on the economic ladder. If one of the essential skills required to move into the middle class in the United States is the ability to use and apply digital information, then can we fairly sit back and say that this is just one more price of progress? Our point is that progress may not be as real or as sustainable when large numbers of people are left out from receiving its benefits. In describing the scope of the problem, we are reminded that the issue of the technology haves and have-nots in education, as with the other divides we have looked at, describe a dynamic evolving problem, not a static one.

Number of Classrooms Connected to the Internet

Just 3 percent of instructional rooms were connected to the Internet in 1994; by 1999, the number had increased to 63 percent, a jump of over 400 percent.

Table 3.1. Poor vs. Wealthy Students per Internet-Connected Computer, State by State*

| | Students per Internet-connected computer in . . . | | | Students per Internet-connected computer in . . . | |
	High-poverty schools†	All other schools		High-poverty schools†	All other schools
Alaska	5.8	6.3	Missouri	12.4	10.4
Arkansas	15.9	11.3	Nebraska	9.3	7.2
California	23.5	18.3	Nevada	29	19.3
Colorado	18.2	13.1	New Hampshire	27	20.3
Connecticut	20	19.4	New Jersey	14.5	16.2
Delaware	8.3	5.6	New York	26.2	12.3
District of Columbia	32.3	31.1	North Carolina	33.5	25.4
Florida	22	15.6	North Dakota	6.4	9.6
Georgia	31	18.4	Ohio	9.8	11.2
Idaho	12.8	10.8	Oklahoma	13.3	13.4
Indiana	17.9	10.7	Oregon	9.4	10.7
Iowa	34.5	9.5	Rhode Island	51.2	16
Kansas	15.4	13.2	South Carolina	13.9	11.4
Louisiana	24.8	25.1	Texas	16.6	13.3
Maine	6.2	11	Utah	8.6	10.7
Maryland	30.4	17.2	Vermont	10.7	11.9
Michigan	24.2	12.7	Virginia	17.8	15.3
Minnesota	11.8	9.7	West Virginia	13	10.4
Mississippi	25.5	23.3	Wisconsin	20	12.2
Montana	11.9	13.8	Wyoming	6.1	10.3
USA	19.2	13.3	USA	19.2	13.3

* Data available on 39 states plus the District of Columbia.
† Based on percentage of students receiving free or reduced-price lunches.

However, despite the overall success of the federal government's E-Rate program (examined in more detail later in this chapter), there remain large differences in Internet connectivity between suburban schools that tend to have larger numbers of their classrooms with access to the Internet and inner-city and rural schools that have far fewer classrooms connected to the Internet. Whereas 39 percent of instructional rooms had Internet access in schools with high concentrations of poverty (with 71 percent of their children eligible for free or reduced lunch), between 62 and 74 percent of instructional rooms were Internet connected in schools with lower concentrations of poverty (figure 3.2).

Ratio of Students to Computers

In 1997, the President's Committee of Advisers on Science and Technology recommended that a "reasonable level for effective use of

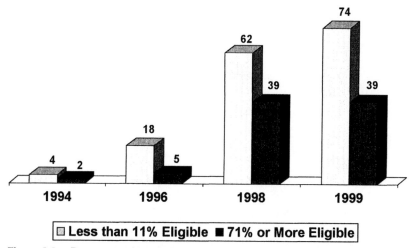

Figure 3.2.   *Percentage of instructional rooms with Internet access, by percentage of students eligible for free/reduced-price lunch.*

computers within the schools" was four to five students per computer. Although the average ratio of students per instructional computer with Internet access decreased from 12 to 9 percent from 1998 to 1999, there are still large differences between schools based on poverty and minority enrollment (figure 3.3). Schools experiencing the most poverty had sixteen students per instructional computer with Internet access, compared to seven among the schools with the lowest percentage of poverty.

Speed of Internet Connection

In 1996, three-quarters of schools connected to the Internet were through telephone modems; three years later, in 1999, the position had reversed itself with 63 percent of schools connecting to the Internet through dedicated lines—but the higher poverty schools still lagged, with 50 percent of schools in this category using the old telephone dial-up connection.

Teacher Ability

Research shows that helping teachers learn how to integrate technology into the curriculum is a critical factor for the successful implementation of technology applications in schools. However, most teachers have not had the education or training to use technology effectively in their teaching. When this lack of experience is compounded with the

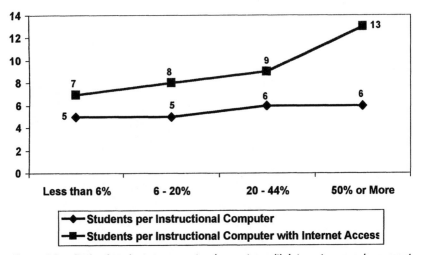

Figure 3.3.   *Ratio of students to computers/computers with Internet access, by percent of minority enrollment in school.*

lack of teacher subject matter certification that tends to concentrate itself in poor urban schools (which already have the hardest time attracting qualified experienced teachers), then the impact in terms of the digital divide in education technology is immense.

For example, we know that in urban schools, over half of the teachers of all secondary teachers who teach math do not have either a major or a minor in math, math education, or related disciplines like engi-

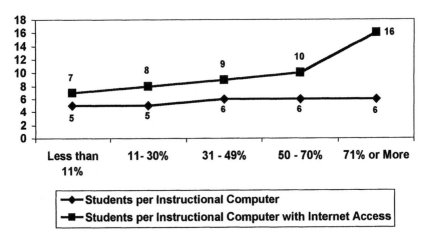

Figure 3.4.   *Ratio of students to computers/computers with Internet access, by percent of students eligible for free/reduced-price lunch.*

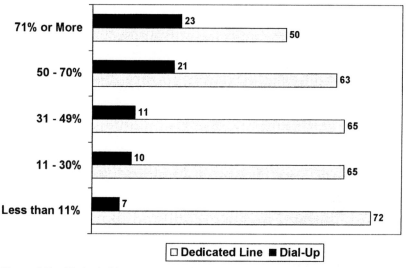

Figure 3.5. *Method of Internet connection, by percent of students eligible for free/reduced-price lunch.*

neering or physics. A quarter of social studies teachers in high-poverty schools, as opposed to 16 percent in low-poverty schools, do not have at least a minor in social studies or related disciplines. Furthermore:

- Only 15 percent of U.S. teachers reported having at least nine hours of training in education technology in 1994.
- In eighteen states, teacher education students do not need courses in educational technology to obtain a teaching license. Only four states require that teachers seeking to renew their licenses be proficient in educational technology.[8]

KEY CHALLENGES OF THE DIGITAL DIVIDE IN EDUCATION

Beyond the issues of technology access and teacher training are five key challenges to closing the digital divide in education:

- A lack of teachers.
- A lack of integration.
- The "last mile" problem.
- The belief system about technology.
- A lack of infrastructure.

Lack of Teachers

As discussed earlier, the problem of uncertified teachers is more intense in high-poverty urban and rural areas where sometimes over 50 percent of the teachers lack certification. Nationally, those teaching without a major or minor degree in their primary teaching subject by state range from 19 percent in Minnesota to 49 percent in California and Texas and 50 percent in Louisiana.[9]

A National Center for Education Statistics (NCES) survey determined that only one-third of teachers reported feeling "very well" or "well prepared" to use computers or the Internet in their teaching. It is therefore not surprising to read that, according to Becker's *Teaching, Learning and Computing Survey*, "computers have not transformed teaching practices of a majority of teachers, particularly teachers of secondary subjects."[10]

This is consistent with another of Becker's observations that only "where teachers are personally comfortable and at least moderately skilled in using computers themselves . . . are computers becoming a valuable and well-functioning tool."[11] We also know that a teacher's professional development in technology and the use of computers to teach higher-order thinking skills are positively related to academic achievement in mathematics.[12]

Lack of Integration

Closely connected with the lack of teacher training is the lack of capacity, not just of teachers but also of the entire school system, to effectively integrate technology into the curriculum. A quick check of some of what might be called the "leading educational technology indicators" suggests that while schools increased their spending on technology by $6.7 billion for 1998–1999,[13] funds spent on training remain paltry at best—only 5.2 percent of that funding was spent on computer training. The king-size portion of the budget remains hardware, with 42 percent spent on new computers and another 20 percent on network installation.

In light of reports from bodies such as the NCES that suggest that the bulk of teachers are a long way from gaining the full potential of the increased investments, only 20 percent of teachers are comfortable integrating technology into classroom instruction. More than two-thirds of principals reported that the major barrier to effective use of technology was insufficient teacher understanding of ways to integrate technology into the curriculum.

Improving Curriculum Material

Elementary and secondary education could take a lesson from higher education, which is now more aware of how new technology poses a threat to a well-established status quo. The Internet can appeal to people with insufficient time and who want the convenience of personalized instruction. Whereas most colleges and universities know that unless they begin to embrace some of the new distance learning technologies, they may not be around in the next few decades, elementary and secondary schools are by and large still debating where technology fits in the curriculum.

But the realities are different for K–12 educators; they do not yet face competition from online schools and have fewer incentives to transform their teaching. The inequalities in supply and quality of school technology as well as training mean that nearly four in ten teachers say their students do not use computers at all during a typical week; nearly three in ten teachers estimate their students' average usage at just one hour per week. And almost two-thirds of teachers say they rely on software or websites for instruction "to a minimal extent" or "not at all."

However, if used effectively, technology can transform student learning for disadvantaged students. A slew of evidence supports the need to move from just simply having computers in classrooms and fast networks to connecting them effectively to a curriculum that can engage students. When this occurs, there can be some remarkable gains — but such a transformation depends on trained teachers.

- Recent analysis of National Assessment of Educational Progress (NAEP) data shows that when exposed to software programs that foster higher-order thinking skills, poor children in high-poverty schools improve their academic skills by one grade level.
- Where technology is well integrated into the curriculum and aligned with standards (West Virginia is a good example), all students have shown improvements in learning.
- Evidence indicates that, when used effectively, "technology applications can support higher-order thinking by engaging students in authentic, complex tasks within collaborative learning contexts."[14]

- In a national study comparing the work of 500 students in fourth-grade and sixth-grade classes in seven urban school districts (Chicago, Dayton, Detroit, Memphis, Miami, Oakland, and Washington, D.C.) with and without online access, results "show significantly higher scores on measurements of information management, communication, and presentation of ideas for experimental groups with online access than for control groups with no online access."

School Budgets

Education budgets should now reflect the major priority: the need for all teachers to know how to use technology to enable all students to learn more effectively. But budgets in high-poverty schools are already stretched in addressing the multiple educational and sometimes noneducational but still vital needs of their students (nutrition, health, drug prevention, security, etc.). What is not often understood is that 50 percent of all poor school-age children live in the twenty-five largest cities or in rural counties.[15]

Nationally, school districts have not invested to nearly an adequate extent in costly areas of professional development (costly in terms of the time teachers have to be out of the classroom and need a substitute teacher; in many urban school districts there are few qualified substitute teachers as well as little money to pay substitutes). It is not surprising that because of so many competing demands, poor school districts have chosen not to invest in professional development to better integrate technology use.

The "Last Mile" Problem

To increase bandwidth for most schools means connecting the school building with an on-ramp to a broadband highway such as that afforded by fiber optic cable or a satellite dish that could connect the school to a local- or wide-area network. A common frustration in many rural communities is that fiber optic networks of long distance carriers pass through or near their communities, but without any means of access. This is comparable to having an Interstate freeway cross your doorstep but with the on-ramp a hundred miles away.

The problems are more than just economic. Not all the technological wizardry that permits high-speed Internet access in urban centers can work its magic in rural areas. DSL lines and 56k modems cannot deliver higher speeds when your school is many miles from the nearest phone-switching office, and cable television companies often leave the more remote spots to the satellite-dish sellers.

Satellite and other types of high-speed wireless technologies would seem to offer hope for spanning great distances and reaching the thinly wired. The cost of downloading Web pages via a rooftop satellite dish is falling. Hughes's DirecPC dish now sells for as little as $299, with monthly service starting at about $30. However, this is one-way technology, and it will not yet serve the needs of many schools.

Belief Systems about Technology

Technology allows students to explore more freely the boundaries of subject areas on the basis of interest and relevance. Students need to be trained to construct more of their own meanings rather than being provided the content through a static and nondynamic source, such as a textbook.

Larry Cuban predicted that efforts to introduce computers into schools would fall short of reformers' hopes, just as experiences with motion pictures, radio, and television had disappointed earlier generations of technology enthusiasts. After an initial gush of enthusiasm, these earlier technologies all ended up being used far less than proponents had envisioned, and the traditional structure of schools remained largely unchanged. Knowledge continued to be seen as consisting largely of concrete subject matter that can be broken into discrete segments and conveyed piecemeal from teachers to students. This may explain why many school computers are kept in closets or sit idle much of the time or are merely used for surfing the Internet.

Lack of Infrastructure

As the Benton Foundation stated,

Businesses generally assume that computer networks require one technology specialist for every 60 users. By that standard, schools would need the equivalent of one specialist for every two classes. But few schools employ any computer technicians at all, even though schools are less able than most businesses to withstand the disruption that system failures and other startup problems can cause.[16]

Notes Tom Carroll, director of the Technology Innovation Challenge Grants Program at the U.S. Department of Education, "If a teacher has planned a science curriculum using technology and the system crashes, she doesn't have time to figure out what's wrong—particularly when she has 30 kids bouncing off the wall." Needless to say, these support issues affect higher-poverty schools more since they frequently lack the budgetary resources to pay for a technician or to outsource the maintenance and repair of computers.

FEDERAL EFFORTS TO BRIDGE THE DIGITAL DIVIDE IN EDUCATION

The federal government's effort to close the educational digital divide takes two primary forms: the E-Rate program and technology funding initiatives of the Department of Education.

The E-Rate

Created as part of the Universal Service Fund for Schools and Libraries as part of the landmark Telecommunications Act of 1996, the federal government created subsidies for schools and libraries of 20 to 90 percent of the costs of basic and long distance phone service and Internet access. The fund also can pay for network wiring within the school and library buildings; however, computer hardware and software and staff training are not allowable under the E-Rate program. In the first two years, the E-Rate allowed for $4 billion in spending.[17]

About 50 percent of the funding went to city districts ($620 million) and about a third ($180 million) went to rural districts. The remainder went to suburban districts or small towns. In the first two years, the largest urban school districts received between $44 and $56 per student. Smaller districts tended to receive a lower allocation, about $29 dollars a student. There was about equal distribution of E-Rate funding between high-minority districts and low-minority districts.

The E-Rate has undoubtedly made a significant difference to the imbalance between high- and low-poverty schools. Applications from the poorest school districts are less than 100 percent and lower than an independent study would have predicted, at least in the program's first year.[18] Whether this is due to insufficient knowledge of the program, limited capacity to afford some of the costs (the costs have to be paid

Table 3.2.   E-Rate Facts

Who is funded?

- California, New York, Illinois, Texas, and Georgia account for 40% of all E-Rate funding.
  - But on a per capita basis, Alaska, Kentucky, Puerto Rico, Mississippi, and New Mexico receive the most E-rate funding.
- Over 83,000 American schools (public and private) receive E-Rate funding.
  - 82% of public schools (over 78,000 schools) receive E-Rate funding.
  - Public schools receive about 84% of the E-Rate dollars.
  - 60% of E-Rate funds go to school districts with more than 50% of the students eligible for free or reduced price lunch.
    - These schools have 25% of all public school students.
- 51% of public libraries receive E-Rate funding.
  - 40% of the E-Rate library funding goes to libraries in the poorest neighborhoods, serving 23% of the served population.
    - The poorest libraries receive twice as much funding per person as the "least poor" libraries.

What gets funded?

- 58% of the E-Rate funds were used for internal connections.
- 34% of the E-Rate funds were used for telecommunication services.
- 8% of the E-Rate funds were used for Internet access.

Despite the general success, disparities remain.

- 74% of the classrooms in the richest schools are connected to the Internet, compared to only 39% of the classrooms in the poorest schools.
- 71% of the classrooms in rural schools are connected to the Internet, compared to only 52% of the classrooms in urban schools.

for in full before a percentage of them, based on the school's child poverty rate, can be reimbursed), or because there are other barriers (such as teachers' capacities and time to integrate more technology into the curriculum) must be left to speculation.

Because the E-Rate does not pay for software, hardware, maintenance, and professional development as well as any "last mile costs," the program's substantive ability to narrow the divide between rich and poor schools must be open to some question.

Department of Education's Technology Initiatives

Federal funds pay for about a quarter of new computers that schools receive, which can be highly significant for high-poverty schools, supporting about half of new computer purchases.[19] However, high-poverty schools have less access to technology than low-poverty schools in terms of quantity, quality, and connectivity. Despite an extra amount of federal funds directed to high-poverty schools, the highest poverty schools received fewer new computers in the 1997–1998 school year (12.6 percent) than the lowest poverty schools (16.4 percent). This fact may explain the disproportionate ratio of computers to students found between high- and low-poverty schools; schools in the high-poverty schools had only one computer for every seventeen students, while low-poverty schools had one computer for twelve students. Computers in the highest poverty elementary schools were less likely to have more advanced multimedia computers (39 percent versus 52 percent) than low-poverty schools or less likely to have those computers connected to the Internet (22 percent versus 34 percent).

Four technology initiatives of the Department of Education stand out as effective programs targeting the digital divide in education:

- The Technology Literacy Challenge Fund
- Star Schools
- Preparing Tomorrow's Teachers to Use Technology (PT3)
- The Technology Innovation Challenge Grant Program

Technology Literacy Challenge Fund

The purpose of the Technology Literacy Challenge Fund is to provide resources to speed the implementation of statewide strategies designed to enable all schools to integrate technology fully into school curricula, so that all students become technologically literate. Technology also can be used to connect teachers and parents to work together; link students to careers, colleges, and community resources; and provide extended learning opportunities for students after school and during the summer.

A key purpose of the program is to enable the states to assist school systems that have the highest numbers or percentages of children in poverty and demonstrate the greatest need for technology. This program provides formula grants to states to accelerate the implementation of statewide educational technology plans by providing financial assistance through the states to school systems. State and local education agencies are encouraged to use this assistance to leverage additional support from business and industry and other public and private entities, including museums, libraries, and institutions of higher education, to use technology to improve America's schools.

Star Schools

The purpose of the Star Schools program is to encourage improved instruction in mathematics, science, and foreign languages, as well as other subjects such as literacy skills and vocational education, and to serve underserved populations, including the disadvantaged, illiterate, limited-English proficient, and individuals with disabilities through the use of telecommunications. The Star Schools program was first authorized in 1988 and was reauthorized most recently under Title III of the Improving America's Schools Act (PL103-382).

Preparing Tomorrow's Teachers to Use Technology (PT3)

The PT3 program supports preservice teacher training related to classroom training. Grants awarded under this program support innovative teacher-preparation program improvements developed by a consortia composed of higher education institutions, state agencies, school districts, nonprofit organizations, and others who are joining forces to develop well-prepared, technology-proficient educators.

Three types of grants are awarded:

• Capacity building grants provide one year of support, averaging $135,000, to 138 consortia that are developing the initial groundwork for an innovative teacher-preparation program improvement.
• Implementation grants provide three years of support, averaging $390,000 a year, to sixty-four consortia that are implementing full-scale program improvements in the preparation of technology-proficient educators.
• Catalyst grants provide three years of support, averaging $640,000, to twenty-two national, regional, or statewide consortia that have the expertise and resources to stimulate large-scale improvements in the development and/or certification of technology proficient educators.

Technology Innovation Challenge Program

The Technology Innovation Challenge Grant Program, funded by the Department of Education's Office of Educational Research and Improvement, helps local communities meet the educational needs of their students through the development of new applications and creative ways to use technology for learning. Local communities are challenged to form partnerships of schools districts, colleges, universities, and private businesses to accomplish their goals.

BOLD ACTIONS/WORKABLE SOLUTIONS

Writing in *Atlantic Monthly* magazine, Anthony Walton asks if a Marshall Plan–type action is needed to address the problems of disadvantaged urban schools when it comes to overcoming the digital divide.[20]

> Mastery of technology is second only to money as the true measure of accomplishment in this country, and it is very likely that by tolerating this underrepresentation in the technological realm, and by not questioning and examining the folkways that have encouraged it, blacks are allowing themselves to be kept out of the mainstream once again. . . . What might be accomplished by an education system that truly tried to educate *everyone* to excellence, not just the children of elites and of the suburbs? Why not a technological Marshall Plan for the nation's schools?

The term *Marshall Plan* is, of course, a convenient shorthand phrase that is sometimes used to suggest that society needs quick and massive government intervention to solve an urgent problem. It is unlikely that the political will necessary to support such a program can be found for a topic as remote as providing better access to technology for poor schools. However, that does not mean that the problem of the digital divide does not require some better strategic long-term thinking and action on the part of the federal government.

When it comes to developing policies to address the digital divide, policymakers have tended to overlook the important compounding effects of family income, ethnicity, and poor schools. Policies have favored offering incentives for the purchase of equipment and telecommunications services (the $2.5-billion E-Rate Program) with a minimal amount of funds reserved for community technology centers ($60 million for multigenerational centers that are intended to promote access to technology in high poverty areas).

Policymakers have largely avoided the issue of how schools can and need to invest in more training for their own teachers and their students' families, providing each with more ability and incentives to use technology effectively. Nor have policymakers addressed how, within a community setting, networking technology could provide greater access to adult education, skill development, and lifelong learning.

The recent commission chaired by Senator Bob Kerrey suggested that the Internet presented a new opportunity to develop an e-learning agenda and that it was now time to "collectively move the power of the Internet for learning from promise to practice." Some of the committee's recommendations include:[21]

- Extending broadband access for all learners as a central goal of telecommunications policy.
- Continuing federal and state support for initiatives and models that make just-in-time, just-what's-needed training and support available to educators.
- Calling upon the public and private sectors to join forces in developing high-quality content and applications for online learning.
- The convening of state and regional education accreditors and organizations to build common standards and requirements for online learning programs, courses, and certifications comparable to the standards required for onsite programs.

Recommendations such as these provide policymakers with greater confidence that it is not only the experts who believe that society is on the verge of a major transformation in education and training because of the Internet.

But what is the reality for poor schools? Schools that may have one or several computers hooked up to the Internet have problems using them—either because the teachers are not trained to use them (most teachers are not) or because they are unable to afford the cost to maintain them.

Should high-poverty schools scrape together every possible dollar to make sure that their children gain access to the latest high-speed computers—even though their teachers might not be trained to use them and the quality of the content is poor? Should such schools make other types of investments, like purchasing laptops, for example? Should schools hire mentors and coaches to work with their teachers, parents, and students to bring them up to speed before making the larger purchases?

As affluent suburban schools now spend their technology dollars increasing the capacity of their computers to use high-speed video and thus increasing their broadband access, poorer schools are still working to improve their telephone dial-up access. Sometimes, such access is made more difficult in inner-city schools because the wiring is old and there are problems with removing asbestos from the walls before installing new wiring. Should high-poverty schools jump over that barrier and go to a wireless solution? What are the costs and benefits of proceeding in this fashion?

The issue of the digital divide in education encompasses the core reasons for the inequalities that minorities face when competing for high-tech jobs. Since we already know from chapter 1 that the statistics regarding the unequal computer ownership and access to the Internet among minority households is quite wide, what schools provide in the way of helping to bridge these inequalities becomes even more important. A focus on the digital divide in education allows us to key in on the conditions that exist in poor, urban, and rural schools and understand to what extent those classrooms in those schools enable students to compete in the new digital age.

Those who argue against a digital divide in education suggest that the reason some poor schools are not taking advantage of digital learning is not because of inadequate resources but because of a lack of interest in digital technology.[22] The possibility also exists that poor schools are slower to move from traditional classroom instruction because they are under pressure to perform well on basic tests. Dabbling with technology, particularly without trained teachers, is risky and only an organization comfortable with how it is performing its core mission can afford to take risks.

The irony of the situation is that these schools will probably return to traditional instruction that has failed. Such classrooms, with their emphasis on basic factual content and with homogeneous student groupings, will do little to prepare students for the world of the twenty-first-century workplace that depends on group work and applying problem-solving skills.

Short of that digital Marshall Plan, there are three main possible approaches:

- Integrated statewide approaches.
- Community-level strategies.
- National standards for professional development and curriculum materials.

Create Statewide Integration Approaches

State governors could take the initiative to come up with a sustainable model for school technology. The governors could argue that the current patchwork of funding, using everything from lottery and bond proceeds combined with annual appropriations, is leading toward chaos. In looking for a more sustainable model—one consistent with the multimillion dollar investments needed to deliver wider bandwidth for high-speed voice, video, and data applications—the governors' advisors might want to examine the lessons to be drawn from various digital or "smart communities."

Blacksburg, Virginia, for instance, has recognized that all residents can benefit from networks connecting residents to government, libraries, universities, and schools. An advisory group might be charged with thinking about what sort of incentives the states might offer to businesses to help create some digital communities. The push may come from a set of states whose governors work to create a larger market for software developers who would otherwise not consider working for the smaller profit margins available normally for content-specific education software. The states may choose to ask the companies to respond to the specific challenges they confront in reaching the standards. The inspiration for what to focus on may come from common problem areas in eighth-grade reading or math as identified by the National Assessment of Educational Progress (NAEP) or perhaps the Third International Mathematics and Science Study (TIMSS).

Governors might request specific "education content providers" that their states are interested in supporting for the development of state-of-the-art materials that lead to specific gains on NAEP-like assessments. They might also challenge the consortia to develop appropriate professional development materials. If the programs are successful, there will be a clear benefit of "going national" with the material.

The fundamental point is that technology should be an important ally for the standards movement; currently, its role is marginal at best. Important opportunities exist in the next century to radically change this state of affairs.

Community-Level Strategies

If the state cannot take on such a massive task, the next logical step is to settle for community-based approaches. For advocates of community-based approaches, the need to respond to the fact that without computers in the home or enough access to Internet-connected computers in schools, high-poverty students and their parents are more at risk of "falling through the net." As Gary Chapman, director of the 21st Century Project at the Lyndon B. Johnson School of Public Affairs at the University of Texas at

Austin states, "It's important for this technology to be embedded in the life of communities." Chapman adds that, for the most part, "people in affluent communities have that technology access at home or in jobs where it is common. Poor people don't have it in either."[23]

A neutral body—a local education or children's group—could convene a technology advisory group and ask to hear from key parties in the technology discussion. Such groups as school administrators, teachers, parents, vendors, and the telecommunication companies could discuss the situation and offer suggestions to improve it. All the data could be displayed on what percentage of the school budget goes to technology and how those costs are divided up among hardware, software, networking, and professional development. It would be refreshing to share that data and to stimulate an honest discussion of what direction the schools' technology implementation is taking.

Then, a serious discussion about two issues, accountability and sustainability, must take place. How can we tell what is working and therefore what is worth spending funds on? What is not working and what do we need to do about it? For example, how do all the more expensive items, which need attention and resources but which frequently miss receiving both (such as professional development and service and maintenance), get their due attention?

The community could also examine some model after-school approaches such as the Boston Club House, detailed in a case study later in this chapter.

National Standards

There are signs that the United States is starting to respond to the need to provide teachers with more efficient ways of finding high-quality Web-based material. *Technology Counts* reports that national groups such as the American Association for the Advancement of Science, the National Endowment for the Humanities, and the National Geographic Society have begun to create an online portal that leads teachers to digital content aligned with the national standards. Moreover, a number of states have set up sites to evaluate "digital content" and its relationship to their standards, while four states have created their own software.

According to the Hudson Institute's Denis Doyle, these developments represent the strength of the free market of ideas, with standards evolving into "superstandards" at the same time as thousands of different instructional units come under the scrutiny of watchdog discipline-based groups.

The question, however, remains whether the national groups will stay at the task long enough and continue to pursue rigorous quality standards to help narrow down the choices that teachers have. To what extent, as those choices continue to multiply, will faction-based groups attempt to jump into the fray and divert attention, energy, and resources away from higher-quality materials? How many teachers will rely on the free market to select these higher-quality materials that may take time to identify, as opposed to just going with a familiar, off-the-shelf, brand-name software?

Incentives to Place Curriculum Materials Online

There are plenty of gifted teachers preparing high-quality content materials, but they do so on a largely voluntary basis without the expectation that they will either get paid for their work or that more than a handful of teachers will use their work. It would be hard for any teacher to sort out the good from the bad within any reasonable time frame.

What sorts of incentives could be offered? For states that wanted to significantly engage the talents of their teachers, it should not be difficult to come up with financial incentives for them to develop digital content and to have the type of quality control in effect that will attract teachers' attention. The state might form partnership agreements with the teacher-developer, and these agreements might help the teacher and the state eventually negotiate with a software company the rights to further develop the concepts and commercialize them.

Standards-Based Reform

We have not yet arrived at a consensus that technology can be used to advance standards-based reform. Even in a state like Texas, which has invested hundreds of millions of dollars in building a world-class infrastructure of computers, less than 50 percent of teachers surveyed for the Texas State Education Agency for the 1997–1998 school year upload or download information; and just 22 percent use the system for collaborative learning projects. Furthermore, only 6 percent of Texas school districts say their teachers use computers in the classroom on a daily basis.

The experts continue to conclude that the lack of professional development has stymied the use of hundreds of millions of dollars of equipment that could be put to more productive use. Can we devise some state-based ways to use technology to help jumpstart efforts? One model that the Public Broadcasting System has developed with the National Council of Teachers of Mathematics deserves some scrutiny. In a project called Mathline, math teachers have access to high-quality videos demonstrating effective teaching of the new math standards. Working with math experts online and in person, participating teachers are able to make the often-difficult translation between the standards as written down in a manual and the way they can be exemplified in a real classroom setting.

Whether or not we want to train the entire nation's math teachers or work the problem from the state or local district's perspective, the costs to develop either a very large-scale or more modest teacher development program are considerably reduced following recent advances in digital technology. For example, it is now relatively inexpensive to send video over the Internet or to publish a CD. We just need to develop the policies that will create the market for the services needed. These policies might be in the form of tax and other incentives a state or consortium of states provides, or ways states and districts might be induced to restructure the spending they now do on the conventional types of professional development that usually end up becoming one- or two-day workshops.

With the advent of many more channels available for use in a digitized television broadcast, the opportunities for television programs to broadcast information for specific audiences and purposes challenges our creativity. We could imagine, for example, a video of an exemplary classroom teacher with separate channels available to broadcast digital content on the particular standards being discussed or commentary by an expert on classroom management.

The fundamental point is that technology should be an important ally for the standards movement, and currently its role is marginal at best.

POTENTIAL MODEL APPROACHES

Moving beyond the hypothetical, there are many working examples of programs that effectively address digital divide issues in education. Presented here are four case studies of programs that can serve as local, regional, and even national models:

- The Boston Computer Clubhouse as a model of an innovative after-school technology program.

- The Appalachian Center for Economic Networks as a model to solve IT support issues for teachers and schools.
- The NetDay Project in Detroit as a model for technology resource and professional development for school districts.
- The United Kingdom's National Grid for Learning as a national model for a clearinghouse of information and best practices for educators.

Case Study #1: Boston Computer Clubhouse

The Computer Clubhouse, [24] created in collaboration between the Boston Computer Museum and the MIT Media Laboratory, is a neighborhood drop-in center where underserved youth from all over the city use the latest computer technology to design and create their own projects. Most of the kids who come to the Clubhouse have never touched a computer before but by the time they leave, technology has opened up new doors for them.

Rather than playing games with computers, the children develop many new skills by learning how to use professional publishing, animation, and design software. Although some of these new skills are computer related, the children also learn to use the technology to express themselves.

The Clubhouse focuses on the individual interests of each young person. There are no general assignments. Instead, when children first come to the Clubhouse, they are able to choose among introductory exploration activities, including designing their own dream house, mixing their own digitized music, and so forth. Later, the children begin to develop more in-depth individual or group projects.

An overriding goal of the Clubhouse is to create a sense of community where young people can safely work together with support from adult volunteer mentors, mostly college students, local company employees, and professors from MIT and many other universities. The Clubhouse is designed to facilitate this community atmosphere. Instead of rows of computers with a teacher placed at the front, the computers at the Clubhouse are placed in pods around the room, and a big green table in the center serves as the "village green." For many kids, the Clubhouse "community" provides a support network for all aspects of their lives.

The Clubhouse is dedicated to offering resources and opportunities to those who would not otherwise have access to them. One program offered is "Clubhouse to College/Clubhouse to Career," which supports the young people in planning for the future and leveraging the technology skills and experience they get at the Clubhouse. Activities include field trips to local companies and area colleges and universities, job shadow days, professional internship and job opportunities, and workshops in resume-writing, interviewing, goal-setting, and educational planning. As Stina Cooke, program developer, says, "Kids who never even thought of going to college are now hanging out at MIT."

Case Study #2: The Appalachian Center for Economic Networks

Teachers, students, and their families at Federal Hocking High School in southeastern Ohio are getting a lot of help these days in learning how to use information technology. This help is coming not from professionals but from other students at the high school. The Appalachian Center for Economic Networks[25] (ACEnet) recently implemented a pilot project entitled Computer Opportunities Program (COP), where it trained thirteen students, eleven of whom had little or no experience with computers, to be the school's computer consultants.

Since being trained, the students have been involved in hundreds of teaching experiences, from instructing other students how to write their resumes on the computer to showing a biology class how to convert data into charts and graphs.

The project's main goal is to train students to be skilled consultants in the working world. In fact, one student is already serving as an intern focusing on computer-aided design systems for a national auto manufacturer's seat cover sewing firm, while another is doing an internship with a computer consulting firm. However, the kids are taking away more than just computer skills. An evaluation of the program revealed that it helped the kids develop time-management skills, increased their self-esteem, and helped them to succeed on the job. The kids found it especially empowering to be able to train their teachers.

ACEnet is a community economic development organization. Although it is located in Ohio, the region's economy and topography are more like nearby West Virginia and Kentucky in that the hills and creeks have been ravaged by long-gone coal mining industries. ACEnet works in the region to create new jobs and business ownership opportunities by linking entrepreneurs and existing businesses with new and emerging markets, with each other, with resources such as training and capital, and with other low-income communities. Community networking is key to its work. As its director, Amy Borgstrom, says, "We envision community networks as integral to transforming our low-income region from a preoccupation with problems to an opportunity-seeking orientation."

Case Study #3: NetDay Project in Detroit's Empowerment Zone

The NetDay project in Detroit represents an opportunity to improve the education in the Empowerment Zone by bringing technology resources and professional development opportunities to the struggling Detroit school districts. The NetDay project in Detroit is unique because it includes two special needs schools. Poe Developmental School and the Detroit Day School for the Deaf, part of the Murray-Wright cluster, are poised to be models for using technology in a nontraditional setting. They have developed the following resources and commitments:

- Copper and fiber optic wiring has been completed in eight different school sites, including two special needs schools—Poe Developmental School and Detroit Day School for the Deaf.
- A pilot PC Upgrade Camp was completed at one of the schools where middle school students learned about computer hardware and how to upgrade used computers. The camp's goal is to increase the amount of computers in the home and in the schools by bringing hardware into the schools and giving children hands-on experience working with computer hardware.
- A partnership with the Office of Educational Technology at the Detroit Public Schools has allowed training for teachers in each of the eight schools.
- MCI Worldcom's MarcoPolo training was delivered to a representative from each of the eight schools, designed to train staff from each school to deliver a training course for using the Internet as a teaching supplement.
- Cisco Networking Academies were offered to teachers in the district, coordinated by NetDay and the Office of Educational Technology.
- Partnerships were developed that will allow six PC recycling centers to be created throughout the Detroit area.
- NetDay involvement has helped secure fifteen area information technology professionals to volunteer their time to help with school and office networking, Internet and computer application

training, Internet communications infrastructure, and technology planning.

Case Study #4: The United Kingdom's National Grid for Learning

Britain's National Grid for Learning (NGFL) is an $80-million plan to make the best digital education content available to all British schools. The NGFL became a signature investment for a government keen to make its mark as a world leader in understanding the transformational power of high tech. With the twin focus on improving the quality of the educational system and on supporting the need to wire every school to the Internet, it attracted a great deal of favorable publicity and leveraged the energy of both the private sector and individual teachers and communities to make it work.

In simple terms, the NGFL acts as an Internet portal with linked sites creating an easy way for teachers and students to find the quality sites and digital content they need to advance the standards. As the government document states: "The NGFL is both an architecture (or structure of educationally valuable content on the Internet) and a program for developing the means to access that content." By encouraging "new models of supply, which free teachers and others to concentrate on their professional priorities," the government hopes to develop a market for high-quality education content available online. The site, for example, has added a number of new functions: a Virtual Teacher Center (where teachers can find first-class curriculum materials), a Parent Center, and links to a growing number of "community grids" connecting public libraries to other local learning resources. The NGFL has set a bright marker down for how to aggressively bring a nation's schools into the twenty-first century.

The government sees a tripling of the market for educational software by 2002 and sees the NGFL as a way of meeting those needs, both online and shortly to be available through digital broadcast. Many interviewed for an October 15, 1999, *London Times Education Supplement* review of the NGFL's progress at that point in time believed that for the National Grid to be a purveyor of "a trusted brand of educational software" in its own right, far more investment should be made in software that the NGFL should then freely make available to schools. Critics believe that the NGFL policy shapers are naive to expect that teachers developing their own curriculum material and sharing their products on the Grid will fill the current void.

What might be some of the NGFL selling points for a U.S. audience? Three clear advantages of NGFL's more systematic approach come to mind:

1. Saving of time and effort in ensuring greater quality control, so that teachers can spend more time on the process of teaching rather than acting as would-be Internet librarians as they evaluate quality and relevance to the standards.
2. Providing incentives and a vehicle for gifted teachers to get their software into the mainstream of customer use and place that work on an equal footing with the products of commercial vendors.
3. Assisting the entire nation's teachers to identify and use high-quality materials on behalf of standards-based reform, opening up ways that other digital content (including video and digital broadcast) can assist teachers to integrate complex media into the curriculum.

Notwithstanding whether the U.K. system is able to realize all the advantages of the system that it has put in place, and the fact that NGFL operates within a centralized education system, there may be elements of the NGFL worthy of emulation in the United States.

NOTES

1. "Online Education 'Increases Inequality,'" *BBC News Online* at news.bbc.co.uk/hi/english/education/newsid_323000/323272.stm (accessed February 8, 2001).

2. Peter Marteka, "Speakers Seek End to Digital Divide," *The Hartford Courant*, February 11, 2001.

3. Daniel Gross, "The Digital Divide," *TheStreet.com*, October 26, 2000.

4. L. Cuban, "Is Spending Money on Technology Worth It?" *Education Week* (23 February 2000); Kulik, J. A., "Meta-analytic Studies of Findings on Computer Based Instruction," in *Technology Assessment in Education and Training*, ed. E. C. Baker and H. F. O'Neil (Hillsdale, N.J.: Erlbaum, 1994; Sivan Kachala, "Report on the Effectiveness of Technology in Schools, 1990–1997," Software Publishers Association, 1998.

5. J. Fouts, "Research on Computers and Education: Past, Present and Future," Seattle Pacific University, 2000.

6. "The West Virginia Story: Achievement Gains from a Statewide Comprehensive Instructional Technology Program," Mann, Shakeshaft, Becker, and Kottlekamp (Milken Exchange, 1999).

7. H. Wenglinsky, "Does It Compute? The Relationship between Education Technology and Student Achievement in Mathematics," Educational Testing Service, 1998.

8. Kenneth J. Cooper, "In Classroom, Widening the Web," *The Washington Post*, December 20, 2000.

9. "Quality Counts 2000," *Education Week.*

10. H. J. Becker, "Findings from the Teaching and Learning and Computing Survey: Is Larry Cuban Right?" Revision of paper written for the January 2000 Technology Leadership Conference of the Council of the Chief State School Officers, Washington, D.C.

11. Becker, "Findings from the Teaching and Learning and Computing Survey."

12. Wenglinsky, "Does it Compute?" Educational Testing Service.

13. Quality Education Data, *QED* at www/qeddata.com/.

14. Means, Blando, Olson, Middleton, Morocco, Remz, and Zorfass, *Using Technology to Support Education Reform* (Washington, D.C.: U.S. Department of Education, 1993). Available online at www.ed.gov/pubs/EdReformStudies/TechReforms/.

15. "School-Age Children: Poverty and Diversity Challenge Schools Nationwide" (Washington, D.C.: General Accounting Office, April 1994).

16. "The Learning Connection: Schools in the Information Age," *The Benton Foundation* at www.benton.org/Library/Schools/one.html#vision.

17. The Urban Institute, "The E-Rate and the Digital Divide: A Preliminary Analysis from the Integrated Studies of Educational Technology," September 10, 2000.

18. Federal Communications Commission, "E-Rate Fact Sheet" at www.fcc.gov/learnnet/ (accessed March 6, 2001).

19. "Study of Education Resources and Federal Funding, Preliminary Report" (Washington, D.C.: U.S. Department of Education, Office of the Undersecretary Planning and Evaluation Department, June 1999): vii.

20. Anthony Walton, "Technology versus African Americans," *The Atlantic Monthly*, January 1999.

21. The Power of the Internet for Learning: Moving from Promise to Practice. This report was released December 19, 2000, at a press conference in Washington, D.C. By law, the commission terminated ninety days after the release of the report.

22. Education World at www.education-world.com/a_tech/tech041.shtml/ (accessed June 24, 2002).

23. *Technology Cybertimes* at www.nytimes.com/library/tech/99/07/cyber/articles/24community.html (accessed February 8, 2001).

24. Computer Clubhouse at www.computerclubhouse.org (accessed February 8, 2001).

25. ACENet at www.seorf.ohiou.edu/~xx001 (accessed February 8, 2001).

CHAPTER 4

The Global Digital Divide

Eliminating the distinction between information-rich and information-poor countries is critical to eliminating the other inequalities between north and south.

—Nelson Mandela[1]

Summary:

This chapter provides in-depth analysis of the global digital divide on both the international (industrialized versus developing nations) and on the intranational/intraregional levels. Specifically, the digital divides in Africa, Asia, the Middle East, Western and Eastern Europe, the Indian subcontinent, and Latin America are discussed. Moreover, Canada, Australia, and Singapore are profiled to examine what the United States might learn from these nations' progressive efforts to bring digital inclusiveness to their societies.

The global digital divide has two forms. The first is the international digital divide, as President Mandela said, between the information-rich and the information-poor counties. The second is the intranational digital divides within countries of the world. The purpose of this chapter is to discuss both the international and intranational digital divides, their core causes, and the lessons the United States might learn from both.

THE INTERNATIONAL DIGITAL DIVIDE

The international digital divide is often viewed as between the United States and rest of the world . . . the United States has more computers than the rest of the world combined.[2] However, the international digital divide is not that one-dimensional. It is not drawn along national boundaries.

Instead, as Mr. Mandela alludes to, the international digital divide is based on the harsh economic disparities between the wealthier, industrialized nations and the poorer, developing nations.

Consider the following:

- High-income countries with 16 percent of the world's population have 90 percent of the world's Internet hosts.[3]
- New York City has more phone lines than the entire continent of Africa.[4]
- There are nearly thirty computers per 100 people in the United Kingdom; in the African nation of Malawi there is one computer for every 10,000 people.[5]

On the most basic level, the international digital divide is shown by looking at the number of telephone lines per 100 people in a region (or nation).[6] The number of phone lines is the leading indicator for the level of universal service in telecommunications.[7] Take, for example, that of the world's approximately 851 million phone lines, 64.5 percent are in located in only thirty* industrialized nations.[8] In contrast, the nations with the lowest gross domestic product (GDP) per capita have only 1.6 telephone lines per 100 people.[9]

Additionally, the number of computers per 100 people is another basic measure of the international digital divide. As table 4.1 shows, with the wealth of the Americas, Europe, and Oceania comes dramatically higher numbers of phone lines and computers.

The interplay between wealth and phone lines/computers per 100 people is even clearer when looking at examples of industrialized and developed nations within the world's regions. Table 4.2 brings the contrast between industrialized and developing nations into sharper focus: the number of phone lines and computers is almost directly proportional to a nation's wealth.

With phone lines and computers as the base, the next level of the international digital divide is Internet access. Internet access is measured in terms of the Internet penetration rate: the percentage of the popula-

---

* The thirty nations are members of the Organisation for Economic Co-operation and Development (OECD): the countries of North America and Western Europe plus Japan, Australia, New Zealand, Finland, Mexico, the Czech Republic, Hungary, Poland, South Korea, and the Slovak Republic.

Table 4.1.   Comparisons in GDP, Phone Lines, and Computers, by Continent

	GDP per capita ($)	Phone lines per 100 people	Computers per 100 people
Africa	823	2.45	.88
Asia	2,144	8.32	2.52
Americas	14,178	33.13	21.34
Europe	12,109	38.48	14.63
Oceania	14,336	40.29	42.71

tion with Internet access. Table 4.3 and figure 4.1 break down the Internet penetration rate for the world's regions.

On the surface, these two tables might appear to point back to the tunnel vision view that the international digital divide is a divide between the United States and the rest of the world. After all, since Western Europe is not a developing region but has such a drastically lower Internet penetration percentage than North America, the international digital divide could not be based on wealth and industrialization.

But a closer examination of Internet usage in specific Western European countries shows that those with a lower level of industrialization bring down the average for the entire region. For example, the

Table 4.2.   Phone Lines and Computers on a Regional Level Industrialized vs. Developing Nations

	GDP per capita ($)	Phone lines per 100 people	Computers per 100 people
Africa			
South Africa*	3,107	13.77	6.01
Cameroon	664	0.66	0.27
Asia			
Japan	30,105	55.75	28.69
Philippines	898	3.88	1.64
Americas			
United States	32,198	66.4	51.05
El Salvador	1,984	7.61	2.01
Europe			
Germany	26,214	58.79	29.69
Moldova	430	12.68	0.8
Oceania			
Australia	18,879	51.97	47.06
Fiji	2,002	10.11	5

* The Republic of South Africa is technically classified as a developing nation, but for our purposes is pegged "industrialized" in relative terms to the rest of Africa.

Table 4.3.   Internet Penetration Rate, by Continent

Region	Internet Penetration Rate
North America	41%
Western Europe	19%
Eastern Europe	3%
Latin America	3%
Asia/Pacific	2%
Middle East	1%
Africa	Less than 1%

high Internet penetration rates of Sweden and Norway (41.28 percent and 44.95 percent, respectfully) are in effect canceled out by the Internet penetration rates of the less-industrialized Spain and Portugal (both 6.9 percent). (See table 4.11 later in this chapter.)

This point is further expressed by looking at the marked contrast in the Internet penetration rates of Western Europe (19 percent) and less-developed Eastern Europe (3 percent). The most striking comparison is, of course, between wealthy and industrialized North America (41 percent) and poorer, developing Africa (less than 1 percent).

Further evidence of the international digital divide being based on a nation's relative wealth and development can be found by looking at the number of Internet hosts and Internet users in each region of the world (table 4.4). An Internet host refers to computers permanently connected to the Internet, such as Web servers.

Again, these statistics show how wealthier regions like North America and Europe dominate the Internet and how poorer regions like Cen-

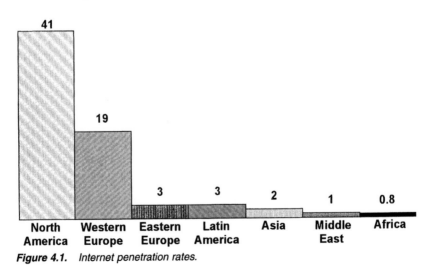

Figure 4.1.   *Internet penetration rates.*

Table 4.4.   **Number of Internet Hosts and Users, by Continent**

	Number of Internet Hosts	Number of Internet Users
North America	80,299,100	194,556,000
Europe	20,309,500	89,066,300
Asia	8,929,770	70,073,600
Oceania	2,062,590	17,227,800
South America	1,264,850	16,593,700
Central America	467,463	1,538,330
Africa	265,366	2,901,450

tral America and Africa lag far behind. This is even clearer when the number of Internet hosts and users in specific countries are compared. The United States has 75,309,400 Internet hosts and 171,661,000 Internet users.[10] Compare the statistics for the United States and those of a poorer, developing country like Peru (4,376 hosts and 321,973 users[11]), and the international digital divide becomes painfully clear.

The final statistical snapshot of the international digital divide in table 4.5 shows the ratio of the world's Internet users to nonusers.

Again, wealthier regions like North America and Europe vastly outnumber poorer regions like Africa and South Asia in Internet access. What these and the other statistics prove is sobering. They show that the wealthiest nations, like the Untied States and Japan, have only 20 percent of the world's population, yet hold 86 percent of the world's income and 91 percent of the world's Internet users.[12] On the opposite end of the spectrum, the 20 percent of the world's population living in the poorest nations, like Ethiopia and Laos, have less than 1 percent of both income and Internet users.[13]

Clearly, the international digital divide is a byproduct of the global economic divide between rich and poor countries.

While the international digital divide splits the world along industrialized and developing lines, there is another component that does not

Table 4.5.   **Ratio of Internet Users to Nonusers**

North American average	1 to 2
European average	1 to 2
Latin America & the Caribbean average	1 to 124
South East Asia & the Pacific average	1 to 199
East Asian average	1 to 249
African average	1 to 249
Arab States average	1 to 499
South Asian average	1 to 2499
World average	**1 to 34**

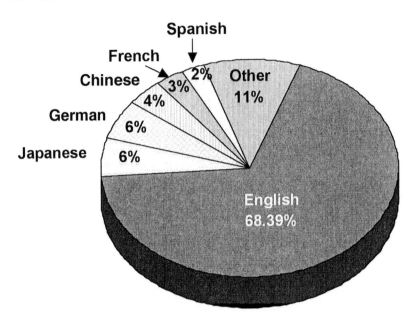

Figure 4.2. Web pages by language.

discriminate based on wealth. Instead, it discriminates based on language. English is used in approximately 70 percent[14] of all websites although fewer than 10 percent of people worldwide speak the language.[15] What good is an Anglophone Internet to the millions—billions!—of people who speak Mandarin, Hindi, or Urdu?

Take, for example, that over a billion people speak Chinese, 332 million speak Spanish, 170 million speak Portuguese, and another 170 million speak Russian.[16] Of the Internet's billions of Web pages, only 3.87 percent are written Chinese, 2.42 percent in Spanish, 1.37 percent in Portuguese, and 1.88 percent in Russian.[17] Without useable Internet content written in their primary language, the Internet is functionally useless for the vast majority of the world's population.

THE INTRANATIONAL DIGITAL DIVIDES

This section gives an overview of the digital divides within the nations of:

- Africa
- Asia

- Indian subcontinent
- Middle East
- Eastern Europe
- Western Europe
- Latin America

In addition, two nations will receive a more detailed analysis because (a) their divides along social and economic lines are similar to the United States' and (b) their governments' actions and programs offer real-world examples of policy solutions that might serve as workable examples in the United States.

- Canada
- Australia

Finally, the most digitally inclusive nation in the world, Singapore, will be profiled.

Africa

It is safe to say that there is no digital divide for Africa. Rather, there is a digital abyss. Africa, with its 780 million people or 13 percent of the world's population, has as many Internet hosts as Latvia (population 2.5 million).[18]

Africa does not lag behind the rest of the world in information technology, it is being lapped by it: in October 1997, the digital divide in number of Internet hosts between Africa and North America was a multiple of 267; in October 2000, this had ballooned to a multiple of 540.[19]

On a regional basis, the most striking digital divide is between the nations of North and Southern Africa, and the rest of the continent. Southern and North Africa are the most advanced regions in terms of information technology use, followed by East and West Africa, with Central Africa trailing the furthest behind.[20] Of the approximately 3 million Internet users in Africa,[21] about 600,000 are in North Africa[22] (primarily Egypt) and over 1.8 million in the Republic of South Africa.[23] This means that there only approximately 500,000 Internet users in the remaining fifty African nations.[24]

The same glaring pattern is true with Internet hosts in Africa. Of the approximately 260,000 Internet hosts on the continent, only 12,000 are outside the Republic of South Africa.[25] Table 4.6 illustrates this "digital rift

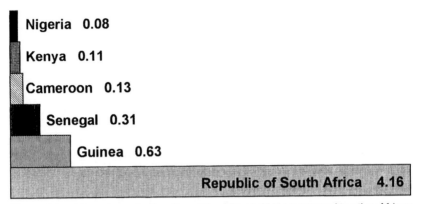

Figure 4.3. *Internet penetration: Republic of South Africa compared to other African nations.*

Table 4.6. Caught between North and South in Africa

	Population	Phone Lines per 100 People	Internet Users	Computers Penetration Rate*	Internet per 100 People	Internet Hosts per 10,000 People
North Africa						
Egypt	68,360,000[†]	**8.08**	400,000[‡]	0.6%	1.12	0.35
Morocco	30,122,000[†]	**5.06**	52,500[‡]	0.17%	1.08	0.73
Tunisia	9,593,000[†]	**8.99**	110,000[‡]	1.1%	1.53	0.03
Africa[§]						
Burkina Faso	11,940,000	0.41	4,000	0.03%	0.10	0.18
Cameroon	15,090,000	0.64	20,000	0.13%	0.27	N/A
Congo	2,940,000	0.77	500	0.017%	0.35	0.01
Guinea	7,900,000	0.59	5,000	0.63%	0.38	N/A
Kenya	30,670,000	1.03	35,000	0.11%	0.42	0.2
Mali	11,230,000	0.25	10,000	0.08%	0.10	0.01
Nigeria	113,860,000	0.43	100,000	0.08%	0.64	0.01
Senegal	9,480,000	2.18	30,000	0.31%	1.52	0.33
Southern Africa						
Botswana	1,620,000	**7.69**	12,000	0.7%	**3.13**	**13.94**
Namibia	1,760,000	**6.38**	6,000	0.34%	**2.95**	**12.06**
Swaziland	1,010,000	**3.12**	3,000	0.29%	N/A	**6.75**
Zimbabwe	12,630,000	**2.07**	20,000	0.15%	**1.30**	**1.80**
Republic of South Africa	**43,690,000**	**12.53**	1,820,000	**4.16%**	**6.01**	**42.01**

* Internet users/Population = Internet penetration rate.
† IDB Summary of Demographic Data, U.S. Census Bureau, May 10, 2000.
‡ Fawaz Jarrah, "Number of Internet Users in Arab Countries Edges towards Two Million," DITnet, March 7, 2000.
§ There are 54 nations in Africa; due to space constraints, all cannot be listed.

valley" between the relative connectivity of North and Southern Africa and the rest of the continent.

On an intranational level, the digital divide is drawn along similar social and economic lines as in the United States—only the divisions are magnified.

- Education: 87 percent of Internet users in Zambia and 98 percent of Internet users in Ethiopia have university degrees.[26]
- Gender: 87 percent of Internet users in Ethiopia, 83 percent in Senegal, and 64 percent in Zambia are male.[27]

Tellingly, one standout in Africa, the Republic of South Africa, also has one of the most divided online societies based on race, gender, age, and income: the typical Internet user in South Africa is White, male, age twenty-six to thirty, university educated, and earns between $24,000 and $45,000 a year.[28] This means that South Africa owes a large part of its online "success" to the legacy of apartheid.[29]

Moreover, many Internet users in African countries are not actually African: 56 percent of Internet users in Zambia are not Zambian![30]

Asia

In the 1980s, Asian nations with emerging, powerful economies were often referred to as "tigers," alluding not only to their economic strength but the economic threat they posed to established economies. This imagery has returned to Asia in 2001. A handful of Asian nations with high Internet penetration rates and affluent populations are now dubbed "Internet tigers."

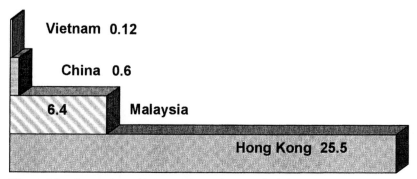

Figure 4.4. *Comparison of Internet penetration rates in Asia.*

But Asia is not all tigers. The reality is that poverty and feeble telecommunications infrastructures prevent the bulk of Asia from going online. Table 4.7 illustrates the huge disparity between the top online Asian nations and the rest of the region.

Even within the tigers of Asia (and some of the emerging "cats"), digital divides exist. Like the United States, it is often age, gender, income, or location that determines who is online or not:

- Age
  - ○ Fifty-seven percent of Internet users in China are between the ages of fifteen and twenty-nine.[31]
  - ○ Forty-three percent of Internet users in Hong Kong are between the ages of fifteen and twenty-nine.[32]
  - ○ Fifty-two percent of Internet users in Taiwan are between the ages of fifteen and twenty-nine.[33]
  - ○ Only 5.7 percent of South Koreans age fifty and over use the Internet.[34]
- Gender
  - ○ Only 37 percent of Japanese Internet users are female.[35]
  - ○ Forty-three percent of the Internet users in Taiwan are female.[36]
  - ○ Forty percent of Internet users in China are female.[37]

Table 4.7.   Asian Internet Tigers . . . and Cats . . . and Kittens

	Population	GDP per capita ($)	Internet Users	Internet Penetration Rate*	Computers per 100 People
Tigers					
Hong Kong	6,800,000	23,593	1,734,000	25.5%	29.05
Japan	126,920,000	34,377	18,300,000	14.4%	28.69
South Korea	47,300,000	8,685	6,823,000	14.4%	18.29
Taiwan	22,260,000	13,392	4,540,000	20.3%	18.07
Cats					
China	1,278,000,000	782	8,900,000	0.6%	1.22
Malaysia	23,260,000	3,607	1,500,000	6.4%	6.87
Thailand	60,620,000	2,038	800,000	1.3%	2.27
Philippines	75,330,000	1,030	500,000	0.66%	1.69
Kittens					
Indonesia	212,090,000	675	400,000	0.18%	0.91
Cambodia	13,100,000	196	4,000	0.03%	0.12
Laos	5,430,000	276	2,000	0.03%	0.23
Myanmar	47,750,000	5,504	500	0.001%	0.11
Vietnam	79,830,000	363	100,000	0.12%	0.89

* Internet users/Population = Internet penetration rate.

- Income
  - In Japan, 49.4 percent of the people in the 10 million yen ($80,000) income bracket are Internet users, compared to only 11 percent in the 3 million ($28,500) income bracket.[38]
  - The average household income for an Internet user in China is $5,780,[39] compared to the average income* in urban China ($708) and rural China ($267).[40]
- Rural vs. urban
  - Japan shares with the United States a digital divide between urban and rural communities: 33.4 percent of residents in the prefectural (state-level) capital cities and 32.7 percent of residents in other large cities have Internet access, compared to only 18.5 percent of residents of towns and villages.[41]
  - Twenty-five percent of the entire online Chinese population resides in Beijing.[42]

The Indian Subcontinent

In an oft-repeated quote, Microsoft Chairman Bill Gates tries to put the global digital divide in perspective by stating that most of the world has never used a telephone, let alone the Internet, and 80 percent of the world lives on less than a dollar a day. "Do [Americans] have any concept of what it means to live on less than a dollar a day?"[43]

While such a thought is beyond comprehension for Americans, for over a billion people in the Indian subcontinent, it is an everyday reality.

As table 4.8 shows, steps must be taken to remedy the region's physical poverty before any thought can be given to its growing "information poverty."

India is an information technology paradox. On one hand, India has blossomed into one of the world's premier software and programming hotbeds with a "seemingly endless supply of software engineers."[44] On the other, it is a country still hobbled by widespread poverty and illiteracy; most of its population is too poor to afford a telephone, let alone Internet access.

First, an outline of India's surging technology economy:

- India exported $5.7 billion worth of computer software products in 2000.[45]

---

* As of February, 2001, 1 yuan = $ 0.120966.

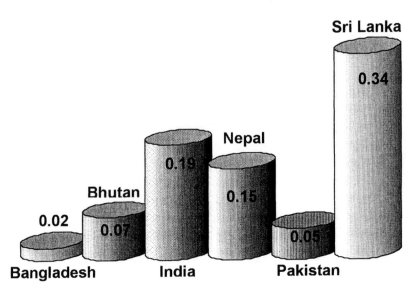

Figure 4.5.   *Internet penetration rates in the Indian subcontinent.*

- Software exports account for a quarter of the Indian economy's growth.[46]
- In eight years, India's annual IT exports are projected to hit $50 billion, or over a third of global software exports.[47]
- India's technology stocks account for 30 percent of the Bombay Stock Exchange's capitalization, up from 8 percent in 1999.[48]

All of which serves as very interesting background when you consider:

- The average Indian citizen earns only $450 a year,[49] or less than $1.25 a day.

Table 4.8.   Substandard on the Subcontinent

	Population	GDP per Capita ($)	Internet Users	Internet Penetration Rate*	Computers per 100 People
Bangladesh	137,440,000	279	30,000	0.02%	0.1
Bhutan	680,000	624	500	0.07%	0.46
India	1,012,400,000	435	2,000,000	0.19%	0.33
Nepal	23,040,000	222	35,000	0.15%	0.26
Pakistan	141,260,000	458	80,000	0.05%	0.43
Sri Lanka	18,920,000	846	65,000	0.34%	0.56

* Internet users/Population = Internet penetration rate.

- Fifty percent of the nation's children are malnourished.[50]
- Forty-eight percent of the adult population is illiterate.[51]

In light of the above statistics, the following telecommunications figures should come as little shock:

- There are only 2.2 telephone lines for every 100 people in India;[52] only 26 million Indians own a fixed telephone.[53]
- Current Internet connections in India are painfully slow: India's total international bandwidth is only 350 megabytes,[†] compared with China's 40 gigabytes and the United States' 200 gigabytes.[54]
- There are 0.3 personal computers for every 100 people in India.[55]
- There are only 2 million Internet users in India, which translates to an anemic Internet penetration rate of 0.19 percent.

Even with such a small Internet population, India still manages to afford a digital divide:

- According to the Internet.in.India study by the Indian Market Research Bureau, the top "A and B [social] classes" in the sixteen largest cities in India represent 1.2 million (67 percent) of all Internet users in India; this same group owns more than one-fourth of all the personal computer in India.[56]
- Forty-nine percent of Internet users in India are between eighteen and twenty-four years old, compared to only 11 percent over forty years old.[57]
- Seventy-seven percent of Indian Internet users are male.[58]
- Seventy-six percent of Indian Internet users have a higher-education degree; only 9 percent are "non-graduates."[59]

The Middle East

The Middle East is one of the most unwired parts of the world. There are only 1.9 million Internet users in the Arab world, which translates into a 0.7 percent Internet penetration rate.[60] In contrast, Israel has 1 million Internet users, which translates to a 15.9 percent Internet penetration rate.[61]

---

† 1 megabyte = 1000 bytes; 1 gigabyte = 1000 megabytes.

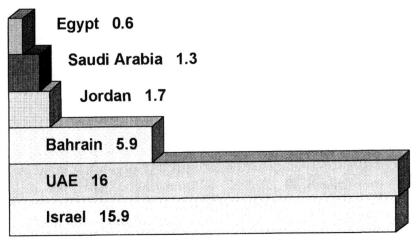

Figure 4.6.   *Internet penetration rates in Middle East nations.*

Moreover, there are only 4.8 computers for every 100 people in the Arab world as opposed to 47 computers for every 100 Israelis.[62] Table 4.9 illustrates the unwired state of the Middle East as a whole and the digital divide between Israel and the Arab world.

Within Arab nations, the tried-and-true digital divide factors of education, age, and gender determine who has Internet access and who does not.

Table 4.9.   Internet penetration in the Middle East

	Population	Number of Internet Users	Internet Penetration Rate*	Computers per 100 people
Bahrain	634,137	37,500	5.9%	10.53
Egypt	68,360,000	440,000	0.6%	1.12
Jordan	4,999,000	25,000	1.7%	1.39
Kuwait	1,974,000	100,000	5%	12.13
Lebanon	3,578,000	227,000	6.3%	4.64
Libya	5,115,000	7,500	0.14%	N/A
Morocco	30,122,000	52,500	0.17%	1.08
Oman	2,533,000	50,000	1.9%	2.64
Qatar	744,485	45,000	6%	13.58
Saudi Arabia	22,024,000	300,000	1.3%	5.74
Sudan	35,080,000	10,000	0.02%	0.24
Syria	16,306,000	20,000	0.12%	1.46
Tunisia	9,593,000	110,000	1.1%	1.53
UAE	2,369,000	400,000	16%	12.51
Yemen	17,479,000	12,000	0.06%	0.17
Israel	**6,270,000‡**	**1,000,000†**	**15.9%**	**47.13**

* Internet users/Population = Internet penetration rate.
‡ "Basic Indicators," International Telecommunications Union, 2000.
† "Internet Indicators," International Telecommunications Union, 2000.

- More than 58.5 percent of Arab Internet users have an undergraduate university degree and 14.5 percent have a graduate degree.[63]
- Seventy percent of Arab Internet users are between the age of twenty-one and thirty-five, compared to only 4.5 percent over the age of forty.[64]
- Only 6 percent of Arab Internet users are female.[65]

Eastern Europe

The Cold War might be over, but many Eastern European nations are still separated from the rest of Europe—except that now it is the digital divide and not the Iron Curtain doing the separating.

Plagued by sour economies and inferior telecommunications infrastructures, many Eastern European nations have Internet penetration rates of less than 1 percent. Yet a few nations have risen above the rest of Eastern Europe to post Internet penetration rates better than many Western European nations (see table 4.10).

As true with other areas of the world, the nations of Eastern Europe have digital divides based on the very common factors of gender, age, and rural location:

- Gender
  - Eighty-one percent of Russian Internet users are male.[66]

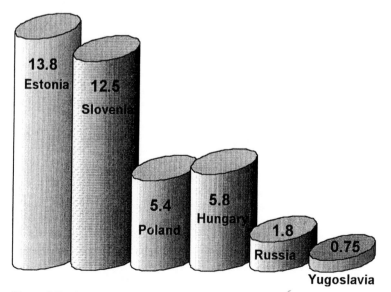

Figure 4.7. *Internet penetration rates in Eastern European nations.*

Table 4.10.   The Best and the Rest in Eastern Europe

	Population	Internet Users	Internet Penetration Rate*	Phone lines per 100 People	Computers per 100 People
Best					
Estonia	1,440,000	200,000	13.8%	35.74	13.49
Slovak Republic	5,410,000	700,000	12.9%	30.67	7.43
Slovenia	1,990,000	250,000	12.5%	37.8	25.14
Best of the Rest					
Czech Republic	10,240,000	700,000	6.8%	37.09	10.72
Poland	38,770,000	2,100,000	5.4%	26.27	6.2
Hungary	10,230,000	600,000	5.8%	37.09	7.35
Latvia	2,380,000	105,000	4.4%	29.99	8.2
Croatia	4,470,000	200,000	4.47%	36.43	6.7
The Rest					
Albania	3,910,000	2,500	0.06%	3.65	0.52
Belarus	10,240,000	10,000	0.09%	25.68	N/A
Bulgaria	8,220,000	200,000	2.4%	35.43	2.66
Lithuania	3,700,000	103,000	2.7%	31.16	5.94
Moldova	4,380,000	15,000	0.3%	12.68	0.8
Romania	22,330,000	600,000	2.6%	16.7	2.68
Russia	146,930,000	2,700,000	1.8%	21.03	3.74
Ukraine	50,460,000	200,000	0.3%	19.89	1.58
Yugoslavia	10,640,000	80,000	0.75%	21.44	2.07

* Internet users/Population = Internet penetration rate.

- More than 82.5 percent of Belorussian Internet users are male.[67]
- Sixty percent of Croatian Internet users are male.[68]
- In Bulgaria, men outnumber women online 2 to 1.[69]
- Age
  - People sixty to seventy-four years old make up only 1.8 percent of the Lithuanian online population.[70]
  - Less than 5 percent of pensioners in Slovenia have access to the Internet.[71]
  - Over 84.4 percent of Belarusian Internet users are under the age of thirty.[72]
  - People fifty-six years old and older represent only 2 percent of the Internet users in Croatia.[73]
  - Only 8 percent of people fifty to fifty-nine years old, and just 1 percent those between sixty and seventy-four use the Internet in Estonia.[74]
- Rural versus Urban
  - Sixty percent of all Internet users in Romania are located in the capital city of Bucharest.[75]

- Almost 80 percent (79.6 percent) of all Internet users in Belarus live in the capital city of Minsk.[76]
- There are twenty telephone lines per 100 residents in urban Russia compared to eight lines per 100 people in rural areas.[77] This disparity between urban and rural telephone lines in seen across the region: in Ukraine, twenty-one telephone lines per 100 urban residents versus seven per 100 rural residents; in Moldova, twenty-three versus six; in Slovakia, twenty-eight versus eleven; in Albania, three versus 0.2.[78]

Western Europe

When speaking of the world's technology "haves," Western Europe is often spoken in the same breath as North America. Granted, while the Internet penetration rate for the United States is 41.5 percent,[79] Western Europe's is only 19 percent.[80] But this could be explained away as a mean trick of averages, as some Western European nations have penetration rates higher than the United States (Iceland, 53.57 percent; Norway, 44.95 percent) that are in effect negated by some laggards (Spain, 6.9 percent).

Thus, compared to the rest of the globe, Western Europe sits up there with North America looking down at the rest of the world trapped in the digital divide.

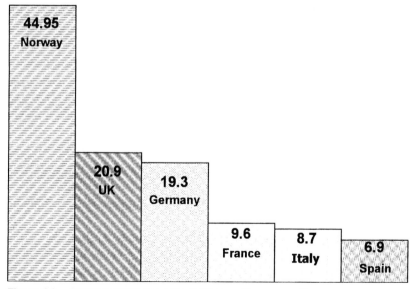

Figure 4.8.   *Internet penetration rates in Western European nations.*

But not so fast. . . .

Several indicators point out that Western Europe as a region is not so close to North America:

- A 2000 study comparing Internet use in the United States and Europe over a two-week period determined that while 26 percent of Americans in the lowest socioeconomic class went online, only 7 percent in the corresponding Western European class did.[81]
- The same study found that 44 percent of Americans in the fifty-five to sixty-four age bracket used the Internet, compared to only 12 percent Western Europeans in the same age group.[82]
- From the same study, the virtual parity among the genders in the United States was confirmed as 55 percent of American men and 52 percent of American women used the Internet; in comparison, 34 percent of Western European men and only 20 percent of Western European women used the Internet.[83]
- The difference in American and Western European women's Internet use can also be seen this way: 50.4 percent of all American Internet users are female,[84] while only 36 percent of all Western European Internet users are female.[85]

Looking at the digital divide within Western Europe, an interesting pattern emerges: the region is almost split evenly between the wired North and the unwired South.[86] On the surface, this North/South divide might be attributed to the income gap between the two areas: as an example, the GDP per capita for Denmark is $26,000 compared to $16,700 in Spain.[87] However, the combination of a lower cost of living coupled with lower taxes in the South (45 percent of the average Dane's salary go to taxes, compared to 20 percent for the average Spaniard)[88] in effect levels the income playing field between the two areas.

The real reason for the North/South divide is an interplay of economic, cultural, and even some argue, climate differences.[89] The central factors appear to be liberalized telecommunication policies in many Northern European nations and the English-dominated nature of the Internet.[90]

With telecommunication liberalization comes a drop in phone charges, thus making it much more affordable for a user in Scandinavia to access the Internet than one in, for instance, France, who pays on a per-minute basis.[91]

And since English is the lingua franca of the Internet, this also benefits the more English-savvy Northern Europeans:[92] while only 28 percent of all Western Europeans[93] speak "some level" of English, 78 percent of the population of the Netherlands speak English as a second language.[94]

Although this divide is not precisely split along a North/South axis and there are individual exceptions, table 4.11 illustrates Western Europe's geographical digital divide. Please also note that in table 4.11 the nations are listed in a very rough approximation of south to north.

Regardless of location within the region, the nations of Western Europe suffer digital divides based on three major factors: income, gender, and age:

- Income
  - Sixty-eight percent of people in the highest socioeconomic group in the United Kingdom have Internet access, compared to 23 percent of the lowest socioeconomic group.[95]
  - Sixty-five percent of households in the highest socioeconomic group in the United Kingdom own a computer, compared to 18 percent of the households in the lowest socioeconomic group.[96]

Table 4.11. South to North along the European Digital Divide

	Population	Internet Users	Internet Penetration Rate*	PCs per 100 People
Turkey	65,700,000	1,500,000	2.2%	3.23
Greece	10,650,000	750,000	7%	6.02
Portugal	10,020,000	700,000	6.9%	9.32
Spain	40,600,000	2,830,000	6.9%	12.18
Italy	57,300,000	5,000,000	8.7%	19.18
France	58,800,000	5,660,000	9.6%	22.08
Austria	8,210,000	850,000	10.3%	25.68
Switzerland	7,160,000	1,761,000	24.5%	46.19
Germany	82,180,000	15,900,000	19.3%	29.69
Belgium	10,160,000	1,400,000	13.7%	31.52
Netherlands	15,960,000	3,000,000	18.8%	35.97
Ireland	3,730,000	440,000	11.7%	32.39
United Kingdom	59,770,000	12,500,00	20.9%	30.64
Denmark	5,330,000	1,500,000	28.1%	41.4
Norway	4,449,000	2,000,000	44.95%	44.99
Sweden	8,880,000	3,666,000	41.28%	45.16
Finland	5,180,000	1,667,000	32.18%	36.01
Iceland	280,000	150,000	53.57%	35.9

* Internet User/Population = Internet penetration rate.

- ○ The highest income bracket in France has a 74 percent personal computer penetration rate, compared to 11 percent in the lowest income bracket.[97]
- ○ Only 30 percent of the unemployed in Ireland are "familiar" with computers, as opposed to 84 percent of students and 64 percent of those in the workforce.[98]
- ○ Only 9 percent of the unemployed in Italy have ever gone online, compared to 70 percent of students and 38 percent of the work force.[99]
- • Gender
  - ○ Only 40.5 percent of French Internet users are female.[100]
  - ○ There are 2.6 Italian men online for every one Italian woman online.[101]
  - ○ Fifty-four percent of women in Sweden use the Internet, compared to 65 percent of Swedish men.[102]
  - ○ Only 33.5 percent of the online population of Spain is female.[103]
  - ○ Only 36 percent of the online population of Germany is female.[104]
- • Age
  - ○ In the United Kingdom, only 15 percent in the sixty-five to seventy-four-year-old age group, and just 6 percent in the seventy-five-plus age group have Internet access, compared to 85 percent of the sixteen to twenty-four year olds.[105]
  - ○ Only 1 percent of Spain's online population is over the age of sixty.[106]
  - ○ Only one-third of people over the age of fifty-five use the Internet in Iceland.[107]
  - ○ Only 14 percent of Danes over the age of seventy has ever gone online.[108]
  - ○ Sixty-six percent of Dutch Internet users are under the age of thirty-five.[109]
  - ○ Only 8 percent of those between the ages sixty-five and seventy-four in Sweden have access to computers.[110]

Latin America

Like the other developing regions previously discussed, Latin America's widespread poverty and enfeebled telecommunications system are the core reasons why it lags behind the industrialized world.

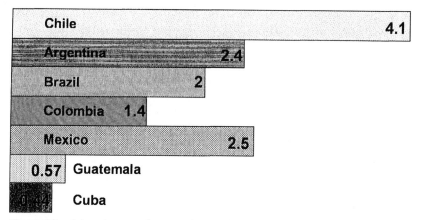

Figure 4.9. *Internet penetration rates in Latin American nations.*

- Only 2.7 percent of the region's population of 500 million own a computer that can access the Internet.[111]
- In an example that holds true for most of the region, 40 percent of the Mexican population[112] live in poverty, only 10 percent have access to a telephone, and just 5 percent have access to a computer.[113]

On a regional level, it appears that a digital divide is growing between the relatively wired nations of the "Southern Cone" (Uruguay, Chile, and Argentina) and the rest of the region (table 4.12).

Table 4.12.   Latin America Looks South

	Population	Internet Users	Internet Penetration Rate*	Computers per 100 People
Bolivia	8,330,000	35,000	0.42%	1.23
Brazil	170,120,000	3,500,000	2%	3.63
Colombia	42,320,000	600,000	1.4%	3.37
Cuba	11,200,000	50,000	0.44%	0.72
Ecuador	12,650,000	25,000	0.19%	2.01
Guatemala	11,390,000	65,000	0.57%	0.99
Honduras	6,490,000	20,000	0.3%	0.95
Mexico	98,880,000	2,500,000	2.5%	4.42
Nicaragua	5,070,000	20,000	0.39%	0.81
Paraguay	5,500,000	20,000	0.36%	1.12
Peru	25,660,000	400,000	1.5%	1.98
Venezuela	24,170,000	400,000	1.6%	4.22
Southern Cone				
Argentina	37,030,000	900,000	2.4%	4.92
Chile	15,210,000	625,000	4.1%	6.66
Uruguay	3,340,000	300,000	8.9%	9.96

* Internet users/Population = Internet penetration rate.

Latin American nations, like almost every other nation in the world, suffer from digital divides based age, income, and rural location:

- Access to the Internet in rural Argentina is almost exclusively limited to the wealthiest 10 percent of farmers and ranchers.[114]
- Fifty-seven percent of the Internet users in Chile live in the capital city of Santiago.[115]
- Sixty-seven percent of the online population of Mexico is thirty-four years old or younger.[116]
- The top three socioeconomic classes (26 percent of the households) account for almost 70 percent of the Internet connections in Chile.[117]

COMMON DIVIDES/DIFFERENT SOLUTIONS

This section discusses the digital divides in Australia and Canada, because their divides follow social and economic lines similar to those in the United States. Moreover, the governments of these two nations have implemented programs that offer real-world examples of policy solutions that might serve as workable examples in the United States. The following section also deals with Singapore, the model for national-level technology-inclusiveness.

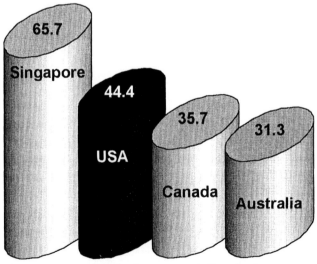

Figure 4.10.   Comparative Internet penetration rates. *

* Calculations for Singapore, Canada, and Australia are based on International Telecommunications Union figures; USA rate from the NTIA's "Falling through the Net" report, October 2000.

Australia

In terms of the digital divide, Australia and the United States are quite similar. First, in regards to who "has" technology:

- Fifty-four percent of Australian[118] and 51 percent of American[119] households have a computer.
- Thirty-four percent of Australian[120] and 41 percent of American[121] households have Internet access.

And second, who does not "have" technology:

- The Australian government has concluded that the digital divide impacts Australians of "low incomes, without tertiary [postsecondary] education, living in rural/remote areas, of Aboriginal and Torres Strait Islander heritage, with disabilities, . . . and aged over 55."[122]
- This mirrors the conclusions of the American government, which found "noticeable divides still exist between those with different levels of income and education, different racial and ethnic groups, old and young, . . . [and] those with and without disabilities."[123]

The similarities between the Australian and American technology haves and have-nots are important because the Australian government has initiated a number of programs to close their digital divide. Since these Australian government programs are aimed at many of the same social and economic groups that are on the disadvantaged side of the American digital divide, it might behoove the United States to use some of the Australian programs as models.

However, before a discussion on the Australian government's efforts can take place, a more detailed review of the commonalities between the Australian and American digital divides must occur, as shown in table 4.13. Once the similarities between the two nations' digital divides have been established, let us outline several Australian government programs that might serve as models in the United States:

- The Networking the Nation (NTN) program with a budget of AU$592 million to upgrade regional, rural, and remote telecommunications.[124]
- The Department of Transport and Regional Services' Rural Transaction Centres Program with a budget of AU$70 million to help small, rural communities establish community access centers.[125]

Table 4.13. Comparison of the Australian and American Digital Divides

Australia	United States
Income	
• 70% of the top income bracket have Internet access, compared to 22% of the bottom income bracket.	• 70.1% of the top income bracket have Internet access, compared to 18.9% of the bottom income bracket.
• 75% of households with an income of AU$50,000 or more own a computer, compared to 37% of households with an income of less than AU$50,000.	• Computer ownership in households in the four income brackets above $24,999* are (in ascending order) 44.6%, 58.6%, 73.2%, and 86.3%; compared to 30.1% for households earning $15,000–$24,999 and 19.2% for households earning less than $15,000.
Education	
• Adults with a "tertiary qualification" [undergraduate or postgraduate degree] are 2.3 times as likely to have Internet access than adults with a primary or secondary education.	• 61.1% of those with an undergraduate or graduate degree have Internet access, compared to 30.6% with only a high school degree and just 1.6% with only an elementary education.
Age	
• Only 13% in the 55+ age group have Internet access, compared to 77% of 18- to 24-year-olds.	• Only 15% in the 65+ age group have Internet access, compared to 75% of 18- to 29-year-olds.
Rural vs. Urban	
• Urban residents are 1.27 times more likely to have Internet access than rural residents (47% in urban areas, 37% in rural).	• Urban residents are 1.08 times as likely to have Internet access than rural residents (42.3% in urban areas, 38.9% in rural).

* As of April 4, 2001: AU$50,000 = $24,366.50.

- The Education & Training Action Plan for the Information Economy with a budget of AU$5 million for an Information Technology & Telecommunications (IT&T) Skills Exchange.[126]
- The Computers for Schools initiative through which 18,000 surplus government computers have been donated to public and private schools.[127]
- The Models of School Teacher Professional Development Project examines "models of teacher professional development for the integration of information technology into classroom practice." The first phase of the project examines "existing models of pre-service education and in-service professional development, both in Australia and overseas." The second phase of the project focuses on "setting up collaborative mechanisms to facilitate the sharing of information

about good practice models through a national network" throughout all of Australia and "across all key learning areas."[128]

- The Farmwide Internet Access for All Project with a budget of AU\$20.3 million "to provide local call Internet access, training, and associated services to all communities in Australia which currently lack such access."[129]

In light of the deplorable information technology status of many Native Americans outlined in chapter 1, perhaps the best Australian program for American policymakers to review is the Open Learning Projects to Assist Indigenous Australians. An important component of this program is an "electronic network linking Indigenous postgraduate students . . . across Australia, assisting them with teaching, research, communication, publication, and information technology support."[130]

A program such as this is desperately needed in the United States when the embarrassing statistics of Native American's participation in information technology studies are reviewed:

- Native Americans account for approximately 0.7 percent of the U.S. population, yet earn 0.49 percent of the bachelor's degrees, 0.25 percent of the master's degrees, and 0.00 percent of the doctoral degrees in computer science.[131]
- In the years 1990 to 1997, a total of six Native Americans earned Ph.D. degrees in computer science, translating to an average of less than one per year.[132]

Canada

Canada and the United States share many things—the longest undefended border in the world, a common dominant language, and (to the chagrin of many Canadians) an ever-increasingly similar culture. Along those same lines, Canada and the United States also share the distinction of being two of the most "wired" nations in the world.

- There are 65.45 telephone lines for every 100 Canadians, and 67.3 for every 100 Americans.[133]
- Fifty-one percent of all Canadians[134] over the age of fifteen use the Internet; 47.2 percent of all Americans over the age of seventeen use the Internet.[135]

Table 4.14.   Comparison of the Canadian and American Digital Divides

Canada	United States
Income	
• 65% of households in the highest income bracket have Internet access, compared to 23% in the lowest.	• 70.1% of the top income bracket has Internet access, compared to 18.9% of the bottom income bracket.
• 79% of households in the highest income bracket have a computer, compared to 34% of households in the lowest income bracket.	• 86.3% of households in the highest income bracket own a computer, compared to 19.2% of households in the lowest income bracket.
Education	
• Only 10% of those with a high school education or less are Internet users.	• 30.6% of those with a high school degree, 12.7% of those with less than a high school education, and 3.7% of those with an elementary education are Internet users.
Age	
• 17% of the 65+ age group use the Internet.	• 29.6% of the 50+ age group use the Internet.

Like its southern neighbor, Canada suffers from a digital divide based on income, education, and age.

Where the United States and Canada separate is in terms of a comprehensive and coordinated set of government programs aimed at ensuring equal digital opportunities. Through its Ministry of Industry, the government of Canada has established the Connecting Canadians initiative to "make Canada the most connected country in the world."[136] The driving principle behind this initiative is the belief "that the Internet is a powerful tool for economic and social development for all Canadians, no matter where they live or how they live."[137]

The following are examples of the many programs of Connecting Canadians that could find a home in the United States:

- The First Nations SchoolNet program overcomes cost and geographical barriers by providing Aboriginal schools with high-speed Internet connections via satellite; currently, this program serves 80 percent of eligible Aboriginal schools.[138]
- The Generations CanConnect program "links seniors and youth in communities across Canada in a dialogue which explores, records, and celebrates seniors' contributions to their country and their communities."[139] The goal of this program is two-fold: first, "by

using the Internet for these projects, youth will acquire technological skills that will help increase their employment prospects"; and
second, "developing seniors' knowledge and skills in the use of the
Information Highway."[140]

- The Community Access Program (CAP) is designed to "help provide Canadians with affordable public access to the Internet and
  the skills to use it effectively."[141] The program's plan calls for
  10,000 public Internet access sites in rural, remote, and urban
  communities.[142]
- The Canada's SchoolNet program focuses on the integration of information technology in education "to help students acquire cutting-edge skills in Internet research and communication."[143]
- The goal of the Voluntary Sector Network Support Program (Vol-
  Net) is to offer Internet connectivity, including computer equipment, Internet skills development, and support to voluntary organizations to "improve the voluntary sector's access to information
  technology and to the skills and tools it needs to play a stronger
  role in Canadian society."[144]

Singapore

With 2,555,850 Internet users[145] out of a total population[146] of
3,893,600, Singapore and its 65.7 percent Internet penetration rate*
stand alone on top of the online world. Almost 90 percent of Singapore
has broadband Internet access,[147] compared to only 4.4 percent of all
U.S. households.[148]

The question for the rest of the world is: how did Singapore do it and
can it be replicated?

Granted, Singapore owes a good share of its online success to having a compact (5,900 people[149] per square kilometer), affluent (per
capita GNP is $39,721[150]), and literate (94 percent literacy rate[151]) pop-
ulation. However, if those were the only three ingredients for digital su-
premacy, why aren't places like Hong Kong and Brunei on the same
high level as Singapore? The answer lies in the role of the central government.

The government of Singapore has made digital inclusion a national
priority. To accomplish this, the government used a two-pronged approach: first, to extend physical access to the entire population and sec-

---

* Internet users/Population = Internet penetration rate.

ond, to take the lead in providing useful, meaningful Internet content to its citizens.

Some the most recent initiatives by the government of Singapore to extend computer and Internet access to its citizens include:

- Through the Singapore Government Network Information Centre, every Singaporean over the age of five will be given a free e-mail address and personal website.[152]
- Thirty thousand low-income households will receive surplus government computers along with free Internet access and basic computer and Internet training.[153]
- The Singapore ONE broadband network will provide free high-speed Internet access to the public via community technology centers and public kiosks.[154]

The second part of the government's approach is just as important as extending access. By making almost every conceivable government agency and service available online, the government of Singapore has made the Internet so indispensable to its citizens that the populace is almost compelled to use it. Central in this strategy is the government's eCitizen Centre. Some of the myriad government services available on the eCitizen Centre include:[155]

- Registering to get married, registering a birth, and registering a death (not necessarily in that order).
- Filing a police report, paying fines, and obtaining legal advice.
- Applying for primary, secondary, and postsecondary education; applying for academic scholarships.
- Scheduling medical and dental appointments.
- Registering a new business, registering for military service, and registering a property.
- E-mailing any government official of any government agency.
- Paying taxes.[156]

While this list could go on and on, covering all the vital and mundane services the government provides online, what is important to remember is that the content is not just information, it is a tool. Consider, for example, that at the website for the U.S. Census Bureau an American citizen can view all the data dating back to the first census. At the corresponding Singapore site, a Singaporean can do the same . . . plus actually fill out his or her census form.[157]

NOTES

1. Mark Atkinson "Dot.force Sets Out Break Log-On Barrier," *The Guardian* at www.guardian.co.uk/business/story/0,3604,407755,00.html (accessed February 18, 2001).

2. Dara O'Neil and Jim Demmers, "Leavers and Takers: Alternative Perspectives on Universal Access to Telecommunications Technologies," paper presented to the 1999 Conference for the Society for Philosophy and Technology, San Jose State University, July 1999.

3. "G8 Plans Hi-Tech Help for Poor," *BBC News Online* at news.bbc.co.uk/hi/english/world/newsid_846000/846146.stm (accessed 18 February 2001).

4. "G8 Plans Hi-Tech Help for Poor," *BBC News Online.*

5. Mark Ward, "When the Web Is Not World-Wide," *BBC News Online* at news.bbc.co.uk/hi/english/sci/tech/newsid_843000/843160.stm (accessed February 20, 2001).

6. Organization for Economic Co-operation and Development, "Understanding the Digital Divide," 2001.

7. Organization for Economic Co-operation and Development, "Understanding the Digital Divide."

8. Organization for Economic Co-operation and Development, "Understanding the Digital Divide."

9. Organization for Economic Co-operation and Development, "Understanding the Digital Divide."

10. Netsizer, "Current Stats for Top Internet Penetrated Countries" at www.netsizer.com/daily/TopCountry.html (accessed April 2, 2001).

11. Netsizer, "Current Stats for Top Internet Penetrated Countries."

12. O'Neil and Demmers, "Leavers and Takers."

13. O'Neil and Demmers, "Leavers and Takers."

14. Nevin Cohen, "Eastern European Digital Divide," *eMarkteter* at www.emarketer.com/analysis/eeurope/20010227_east_europe.html (accessed March 1, 2001).

15. The United Nations Development Programme, "The UNDP World Development Report, 2000" at www.undp.org/hdro/ (accessed March 12, 2001).

16. Summer Institute of Languages, "Ethnologue: Languages of the World, 1999."

17. Cohen, "Eastern European Digital Divide."

18. Mike Jensen, "African Internet Status," *Information and Communication Technologies, Internet and Computer Infrastructure in Africa*, at www3.sn.apc.org/africa/afstat.htm (accessed March 18, 2001).

19. Organization for Economic Co-operation and Development, "Understanding the Digital Divide."

20. Jensen, "African Internet Status."

21. Netsizer, "Current Stats for Top Internet Penetrated Countries."

22. Jensen, "African Internet Status."

23. Media Africa.com, "Fourth South African Internet Services Industry Survey 2000," *Media Africa.com*, May 23, 2000.

24. Jensen, "African Internet Status."

25. Jensen, "African Internet Status."

26. Jensen, "African Internet Status."

27. Jensen, "African Internet Status."

28. Jensen, "African Internet Status."

29. Jensen, "African Internet Status."

30. Jensen, "African Internet Status."

31. Imasia, "Survey Shows 24 Million Internet Users in Greater China" at www.iamasia.com/presscentre/pressrel/pressrel_news.cfm?content_id=398 (accessed February 12, 2001).

32. Imasia, "Survey Shows 24 Million Internet Users in Greater China."

33. Imasia, "Survey Shows 24 Million Internet Users in Greater China."

34. "Korean Internet Users Top 19M in 2000," *InternetNews.com*, January 22, 2001.

35. NUA Internet Surveys, "Only a Third of Japanese Users Are Women" at www.nua.ie/surveys/index.cgi?f=VS&art_id=905355820&rel=true (accessed December 30, 2000).

36. Imasia, "Survey Shows 24 Million Internet Users in Greater China."

37. Imasia, "Survey Shows 24 Million Internet Users in Greater China."

38. "Digital Divide Widens in Japan: Survey," *asianbiztech.com*, November 8, 2000.

39. Imasia, "Survey Shows 24 Million Internet Users in Greater China."

40. Consulate General of the People's Republic of China, Houston, Texas, *www.chinahouston.org* (1 yuan = $0.1209 as of February 2001).

41. "Digital Divide Widens in Japan: Survey," *asianbiztech.com*, November 8, 2000.

42. Catherine L. Mann "The Future of the Internet in China," *Institute for International Economics*, November 15, 1999.

43. Manny Frischberg, "Gates: Poor Need Meds, not PCs," *Wired News*, October 19, 2000.

44. Eddie Cheung, "Profiling Indian Internet Users: Part 1," *eMarketer*, January 4, 2001.

45. "Great Indian Digital Divide," *The Hindustan Times* at www.hindustantimes.com/nonfram/290600/detOPI03.htm (accessed March 8, 2001).

46. "Great Indian Digital Divide," *The Hindustan Times*.

47. "Great Indian Digital Divide," *The Hindustan Times*.

48. "Great Indian Digital Divide," *The Hindustan Times*.

49. NUA Internet Surveys, "India Pushes IT Development in Rural Villages" at www.nua.ie/surveys/index.cgi?f=VS&art_id=905356361&rel=true (accessed January 25, 2001).

50. NUA Internet Surveys, "India Pushes IT Development in Rural Villages."

51. UNESCO and the Asia/Pacific Cultural Centre for UNESCO (ACCU) at www.accu.or.jp/litdbase/stats/index.htm (accessed March 8, 2001).

52. Eddie Cheung, "Profiling Indian Internet Users: Part 1."

53. "Bridging the Digital Divide," *BBC News Online* at news.bbc .co.uk/hi/english/business/newsid_1119000/1119936.stm (accessed March 5, 2001).

54. NUA Internet Surveys, "IT in India Thwarted by Poor Infrastructure."

55. Eddie Cheung, "Profiling Indian Internet Users: Part 1."

56. Uday Lal Pai, "Forty Percent of Homes in India Will Be Net-enabled" at *asia.internet.com*, asia.internet.com/cyberatlas/2001/0208-india.html (accessed March 15, 2001).

57. Cheung, "Profiling Indian Internet Users: Part 1."

58. Cheung, "Profiling Indian Internet Users: Part 1."

59. Cheung, "Profiling Indian Internet Users: Part 1."

60. Fawaz Jarrah, "Number of Internet Users in Arab Countries Edges towards Two Million," *DITnet* at www.ditnet.co.ae/itnews/internet.html (accessed March 7, 2001).

61. International Telecommunications Union, "Internet Indicators."

62. International Telecommunications Union, "Internet Indicators."

63. Jarrah, "Number of Internet Users in Arab Countries."

64. Jarrah, "Number of Internet Users in Arab Countries."

65. Jarrah, "Number of Internet Users in Arab Countries."

66. NUA Internet Surveys, "Russian Internet Audience Increases" at www.nua.ie/surveys/index.cgi?f=VS&art_id=905356000&rel=true (accessed March 15, 2001).

67. Embassy of the Republic of Belarus to the United States, "Belarus: Overview of Internet Economy," March 5, 2001.

68. NUA Internet Surveys, "Internet No-Go in Croatia" at www.nua.ie/ surveys/index.cgi?f=VS&art_id=905356041&rel=true (accessed March 15, 2001).

69. Dessislava Damianova, "24% of Bulgarians Use the Internet Daily," *europemedia.net*, January 16, 2001.

70. Baltic News Service "Number of Internet Users Rises Slightly," *europemedia.net*, January 29, 2001.

71. Vasja Vehovar, "The Digital Divide in Slovenia," *europmedia.net*, January 24, 2001.

72. Embassy of the Republic of Belarus to the United States, "Belarus: Overview of Internet Economy."

73. NUA Internet Surveys, "Internet No-Go in Croatia."

74. "Internet Users among Population of Estonia," BMF Gallup Media (Tallinn, Estonia, August 10, 2000).

75. Vlad Popovici, "Good News for Internet Development in Romania," *europemedia.net*, February 1, 2001.

76. Embassy of the Republic of Belarus to the United States, "Belarus: Overview of Internet Economy."

77. Global Internet Liberty Campaign, "Bridging the Digital Divide: Internet Access in Central and Eastern Europe" at www.cdt.org/international/ceeaccess/ (accessed March 15, 2001).

78. Global Internet Liberty Campaign, "Bridging the Digital Divide."

79. National Telecommunications and Information Administration, *Falling through the Net* (Washington, D.C.: U. S. Department of Commerce).

80. Jupiter Communications, July 2000.

81. NUA Internet Surveys, "Europe: Fewer Users, Greater Divide Than U.S." at www.nua.ie/surveys/index.cgi?f=VS&art_id=905356195&rel=true (accessed March 10, 2001).

82. NUA Internet Surveys, "Europe."

83. NUA Internet Surveys, "Europe."

84. Alec Klein and Carrie Johnson, "Women Surf Past Men on Net," *The Washington Post*, August 10, 2000.

85. NUA Internet Surveys, "Digital Divide Persists in Europe" at www.nua.ie/surveys/index.cgi?f=VS&art_id=905355818&rel=true (accessed March 15, 2001).

86. Marius Meland, "A Tale of Two Worlds" at www.forbes.com/2000/05/23/feat2.html (accessed March 23, 2001).

87. Meland, "A Tale of Two Worlds."

88. Meland, "A Tale of Two Worlds."

89. Forrester Research, "Latin Culture and Climate Explain Low Internet Adoption in France, Italy and Spain," August 15, 2000.

90. Meland, "A Tale of Two Worlds."

91. Meland, "A Tale of Two Worlds."

92. Meland, "A Tale of Two Worlds."

93. "The eEurope Report," *eMarketer*, September 7, 1999.

94. NUA Internet Surveys, "Digital Dutch Are Fervent Internet Users" at www.nua.ie/surveys/index.cgi?f=VS&art_id=905356355&rel=true (accessed March 15, 2001).

95. "Digital Divisions Split Britain," *BBC News Online* at news.bbc.co.uk/hi/english/education/newsid_1143000/1143065.stm (accessed March 8, 2001).

96. "Deprived Homes to Go Online," *BBC News Online* at news.bbc.co.uk/hi/english/education/newsid_716000/716395.stm (accessed March 17, 2001).

97. "Bridging the Digital Divide," *BBC News Online* at news.bbc.co.uk/hi/english/business/newsid_1119000/1119936.stm (accessed March 5, 2001).

98. Information Society Commission (Ireland), at www.irlgov.ie/taoiseach/publication/infosocactionplan/infosoc.htm (accessed March 14, 2001).

99. NUA Internet Surveys, "Women Driving Italian Internet Boom" at www.nua.ie/surveys/index.cgi?f=VS&art_id=905356139&rel=true (accessed March 15, 2001).

100. NUA Internet Surveys, "Constant Growth for French Net Population" www.nua.ie/surveys/index.cgi?f=VS&art_id=905356222&rel=true (accessed March 15, 2001).

101. NUA Internet Surveys, "Women Driving Italian Internet Boom."

102. eMarketer, "The Quick eStats Newsletter," March 20, 2001.

103. Marta Iglesias, "Spain Still Lags behind Europe in Internet Penetration," *europemedia.net*, March 15, 2001.

104. NUA Internet Surveys, "Internet Use Varies across Europe" at www.nua.ie/surveys/index.cgi?f=VS&art_id=905356143&rel=true (accessed March 8, 2001).

105. "Deprived Homes To Go Online," *BBC News Online*.

106. Marta Iglesias, "Spain Still Lags Behind Europe in Internet Penetration."

107. NUA Internet Surveys, "Vast Majority of Icelanders Are Online" at www.nua.ie/surveys/index.cgi?f=VS&art_id=905355921&rel=true (accessed March 15, 2001).

108. NUA Internet Surveys, "Sixty Percent of Danish Adults Online" at www.nua.ie/surveys/index.cgi?f=VS&art_id=905355903&rel=true (accessed March 15, 2001).

109. NUA Internet Surveys, "Digital Dutch Are Fervent Internet Users."

110. Araine Sains, "Sweden's Digital Divide," *Europe*, December 2000.

111. NUA Internet Surveys, "Lat Am Net Growth Has to be Faster, Fairer" at www.nua.ie/surveys/index.cgi?f=VS&art_id=905355715&rel=true (accessed March 18, 2001).

112. Andrew Hurst, "Mexico's Fox Outlines Internet Vision," *dailynews.yahoo.com* at dailynews.yahoo.com/h/nm/20010317/wr/mexico_fox_dc_1.html (accessed March 21, 2001).

113. Julia Scheeres, "In Mexico, Net Not a Priority," *Wired News*, January 16, 2001.

114. NUA Internet Surveys, "Argentina: IT and Internet Growth Continue" at www.nua.ie/surveys/index.cgi?f=VS&art_id=905356015&rel=true (accessed March 21, 2001).

115. NUA Internet Surveys, "Digital Divide Evident in Chile" at www.nua.ie/surveys/index.cgi?f=VS&art_id=905356180&rel=true (accessed March 17, 2001).

116. NUA Internet Surveys, "Young Mexicans Get Wired—Not Wireless" at www.nua.ie/surveys/index.cgi?f=VS&art_id=905356420&rel=true (accessed March 21, 2001).

117. NUA Internet Surveys, "Digital Divide Evident in Chile."

118. Australian Bureau of Statistics, "Internet Use of the Internet and Home Computers" at www.noie.gov.au/projects/access/community/digitaldivide/Digitaldivide.htm (accessed March 15, 2001).

119. National Telecommunications and Information Administration, *Falling through the Net*.

120. Australian Bureau of Statistics, "Internet Use of the Internet and Home Computers."

121. National Telecommunications and Information Administration, *Falling through the Net.*

122. The National Office for the Information Economy (Australia), at www.noie.gov.au (accessed March 15, 2001).

123. National Telecommunications and Information Administration, "Executive Summary of the 'Falling through the Net: Toward Digital Inclusion' Report" (Washington, D.C.: U.S. Department of Commerce, October 2000).

124. The National Office for the Information Economy (Australia).

125. The National Office for the Information Economy (Australia).

126. The National Office for the Information Economy (Australia).

127. The National Office for the Information Economy (Australia).

128. The National Office for the Information Economy (Australia).

129. The National Office for the Information Economy (Australia).

130. The National Office for the Information Economy (Australia).

131. Oscar N. Garcia, "Researching Foundations on Successful Participation of Underrepresented Minorities in Information Technology" (Wright University, November 1999).

132. Garcia, "Researching Foundations on Successful Participation of Underrepresented Minorities in Information Technology."

133. International Telecommunication Union, "Basic Indicators."

134. "eStats Newsletter," *eMarketer.com,* March 29, 2001.

135. National Telecommunications and Information Administration, *Falling through the Net.*

136. Government of Canada, *Connecting Canadians*, at www.connect.gc .ca/ (accessed March 18, 2001).

137. Government of Canada, *Connecting Canadians.*

138. First Nations SchoolNet, at www.schoolnet.ca/aboriginal/ (accessed March 18, 2001).

139. Government of Canada, *Connecting Canadians.*

140. Government of Canada, *Connecting Canadians.*

141. Government of Canada, *Connecting Canadians.*

142. Government of Canada, *Connecting Canadians.*

143. Government of Canada, *Connecting Canadians.*

144. Government of Canada, *Connecting Canadians.*

145. Netsizer, "Current Stats for Top Internet Penetrated Countries."

146. Singapore Department of Statistics, 2001.

147. NUA Internet Surveys, "Singapore Is Role Model for eGovernment" at www.nua.ie/surveys/index.cgi?f=VS&art_id=905356237&rel=true (accessed March 20, 2001).

148. National Telecommunications and Information Administration, *Falling through the Net.*

149. Singapore Department of Statistics, 2001.

150. Singapore Department of Statistics, 2001.

151. Singapore Department of Statistics, 2001.

152. Adam Creed, "Singapore to Fund Citizen's Internet Access," *Newsbytes*, March 1, 2000.

153. Creed, "Singapore to Fund Citizen's Internet Access."

154. Creed, "Singapore to Fund Citizen's Internet Access."

155. eCitizen Centre, at www.gov.sg (accessed March 20, 2001).

156. NUA Internet Surveys, "Singapore Is Role Model for eGovernment."

157. Casuarina Peck, "Singapore Scores First in Use of Net for Census," *Singapore.internet.news.com*, February 2, 2000.

CHAPTER 5

Policy Options for Closing the Digital Divide

A rudimentary PC costs as much as a color television and an Internet connection costs somewhere between zero and one-half the cost of a cable television subscription. Everyone has a color TV (or two or three) and 70 percent of households have cable television. Universal television is here, and universal Internet appears to be on the way without direct government subsidies.

—Robert W. Crandall, The Brookings Institution[1]

For every complex problem, there is a solution that is simple, neat, and wrong.

—H. L. Mencken

Summary:

This chapter objectively presents the four major policy options to close the digital divide. Within the discussion of each option, real-world, working examples are given. The four main options are the market solution, governmental action, philanthropy/community action, and private/public partnerships.

The focus of this chapter is to present the four main policy options that have been offered to solve the digital divide. The goal of this chapter is to objectively discuss the rationales behind the policy options and to give examples of the options being implemented. The four main policy options are:

1. Let the market fix the problem.
2. Governmental action.

3. Rely on philanthropy and community action.
4. Private/public partnerships.

OPTION 1: LET THE MARKET FIX THE PROBLEM

To bridge the digital divide, the basic laws of supply and demand should be the primary engines for change, not governmental action. The government's role (if any) should only be to nurture competition and fund basic research.[2]

Instead of government meddling, the real solution to the digital divide lies in allowing the market to fix the problem. The pro-market approach says that, in a time of virtually free computers and Internet access, government intervention to close the digital divide is happening too late and is a waste of taxpayer's money.[3] Furthermore, governmental intervention will soon become interference. Government programs and subsidies will soon be followed by the government's regulatory hand in such matters as online privacy, content controls, taxes, and access fees.[4] As a matter of fact, government involvement will not speed Internet access to those without it. Instead, it will slow down "the natural evolution of e-commerce and reduce the quality and range of services everyone has the right to expect."[5]

Policymakers should be patient and let the market fulfill consumers' evolving needs instead of rushing to create expensive and unwarranted new federal programs.[6] It is a simple historic fact that new technologies spread slowly. First, the wealthy get the technology, then the middle classes, and finally the poor, but eventually everyone gets the technology.

And, it seems, the newer the technology, the quicker it spreads.[7] For example, it took forty-six years for a quarter of the American population to get electricity while it took thirty-five years for a quarter of the population to get telephone service. Yet it just took sixteen years for a quarter of American households to get a personal computer and only seven years for a quarter to get Internet access.[8] The free market proponents therefore claim that the digital divide is not a question of haves and have-nots, but of have-nows and have-laters.[9] As the Internet technology marketplace matures, prices will fall even more, making Internet access affordable to all who want it.

The basic forces of supply and demand have driven the price of a personal computer down to the level of a television set and the monthly price of Internet access *lower* than the monthly price of cable television.[10] Further, the market is driving the cost of Internet access even lower. From October 1999 to September 2000, the average cost of Internet access for twenty hours per month at peak times fell by 24 percent, and 21 percent at off-peak times; for forty hours of peak usage it fell 27 percent, and 26 percent at off-peak.[11]

Examples of the Market Option in Action

Specifically, there are three ways that the market is closing the digital divide by providing inexpensive or even free options to gain computer and Internet access.

1. *Inexpensive and even free computers are readily available.*[12] The price of a basic home computer has plummeted over time. Granted, the price for the latest PC with the fastest processor and all the cutting-edge bells and whistles is still prohibitively expensive for many consumers (over $2000 for an Intel Pentium 4 1.4 gigahertz computer).[13] However, for a basic unit that will allow the user to access the Internet, do word processing, and create a Web page and all the other "necessities," the price is drastically more affordable:

   - $295 for a 500-megahertz Intel Celeron processor-powered computer with 20-gigabyte hard drive[14]
   - $302 for a 600-megahertz Intel Celeron processor-powered computer with a 10-gigabyte hard drive[15]
   - $396 for 750-megahertz Intel Pentium 3 processor-powered computer with a 10-gigabyte hard drive[16]

   Why is the price of these computers so much more affordable? Simple—because of heavy market competition.[17]
   Moreover, as the above prices show, many entry-level computers are cheaper than a new television set, which brings up an obvious question: with 98.7 percent of all Americans (including 97.3 percent of all poor households) owning a TV, how real is the digital divide if you can buy an Internet-ready computer for less than a television set?[18]
   For those who cannot afford even a $300 computer, some companies offer free computers. Take, for example, FreeDesktops .com. They offer a 566-megahertz Intel Celeron-powered

computer with a 20-gigabyte hard drive, as their name implies, for free.[19] If a user is willing to put up with advertisements on the screen, the computer is theirs at absolutely no charge.[20]

2. *Like computers, Internet access can be cheap and even free.*[21] Just as the market has provided free computers to those who want it, there are a slew of companies that offer free Internet access. Companies like NetZero, Juno, and DotNow.com provide free Internet access. These free services are supported by advertisements placed on the user's Web browser.

3. *Companies provide free computer and Internet applications.*[22] Once a user has connected the free computer to the free Internet access, there is wealth of free computing and Internet applications available.

- Companies like FreeDiskSpace.com offer free storage of computer files.[23]
- Free e-mail (or more specifically "Web-mail") is available by a host of companies like Hotmail, Yahoo!, and Netscape.
- Companies like CyberTechHelp.com offer technical support for computer and Internet questions or problems free-of-charge.[24]
- Computer software can be downloaded completely free (and legally) at places like Download.com or FreewareFiles.com.

OPTION 2: GOVERNMENT ACTION

On the opposite side of the digital debate from the pro-market voices are those who believe that the digital divide is a serious enough problem to warrant governmental involvement. This opinion has been manifested in two possible options for solving the digital divide through governmental action: first, attack the digital divide like any other pressing social and economic problem by using federal, state, and local funds to come up with solutions; and second, solve the digital divide through proactive federal, legal, regulatory, and tax policies.

For such a huge social and economic problem like the digital divide, it is foolhardy to assume any meaningful solution can be found without the active participation and leadership of the government. After all, did the market build the interstate highway system or raise the literacy rate or put a man on the moon?[25] No, the government shouldered these awesome responsibilities, just as it should with the digital divide.[26] The American people appear to be behind this crusade: 57 percent said that the government should "help low-income get access to computers and the Internet."[27]

One of the strongest arguments of the pro-market faction is the comparison of the gradual spread of access to television over the past decades to the eventual spread of Internet access in the near future. Yet noted author Don Tapscott counters this with an updated "apples and oranges" rebuttal. He points out that television "is basically a passive form of entertainment. . . . The new media [the Internet] require the active, informed, literate participation of a user."[28] Therefore, Tapscott explains, the spread of television access will not be replicated by the Internet, which takes deliberate effort by literate and motivated users, as opposed the inherently passive nature of television.[29] Our society cannot rely on the market to bridge the digital divide; we must look to the government to do so.

This view is best expressed in the 2001 report "Using Information Technology to Transform the Way We Learn" by the President's Information Technology Advisory Committee (PITAC). As PITAC's name implies, it is the executive-level group that advises President George W. Bush on information technology issues. The PITAC report calls for "the Federal government to make the integration of information technology with education and training a national priority."[30]

Examples of Federally Funded Programs

One of the most interesting examples of governmental funding on the federal level is the Department of the Labor's awards of $12.4 million in grants to train U.S. IT workers. An additional $40 million will be used to fund projects to train workers in local markets. Funds for these efforts come from the filing fees of the controversial H-1B visa.[31] As mentioned earlier, the H-1B visa is the vehicle used by as many 115,000 foreign workers a year to gain positions in the domestic IT industry. So, the federal government is using the funds generated from what is called a main factor in the growing digital divide in IT training (the H-1B visa program) to help foster a new generation of American IT workers.

Other examples of federal funding include the $135 million in grants provided by the Department of Education to train 400,000 teachers to use information technologies more effectively in the classroom[32] and the Kids 2000 program. Kids 2000 will provide each of the 2,300 Boys and Girls Clubs in America an average of ten computers.[33] In addition, Kids 2000 will provide every Boys and Girls Club with Internet access and instructors to show the youths how to utilize the technology.[34]

Other notable examples include:

- President George W. Bush's proposal for a $3-billion fund for information technology for schools and libraries on top of $400 million to establish and maintain more than 2,000 community centers around the nation to provide free Internet access, computer literacy training, and professional skills development.[35] In addition, President Bush is looking to provide $15 million annually to establish the Education and Technology Clearinghouse to make information on education technology programs, best practices, and the latest research studies available to states and schools.[36]
- To combat the emerging broadband divide, Senator Hillary Clinton has proposed a bill that would allow rural communities to use bonds to finance broadband services, issue grants to encourage companies to extend broadband networks to rural areas, and use the National Science Foundation to develop new broadband technologies specifically targeting remote areas.[37]
- Senator Tom Harkin's Technology for All Americans Act of 2000 aims at closing the digital divide for people with disabilities by awarding grants to:
  - States to "improve electronic information technology accessibility, including computers and Internet access, at public libraries."[38]
  - Institutions of higher education "for incorporating the design and use of accessible technology into curricula for certain academic and professional programs."[39]
  - State education agencies "for demonstration projects to promote the incorporation of technology into education, and transition from school to work, of children with disabilities to increase their independence and self-sufficiency."[40]

Examples of Federal Regulations and Tax Policy

An alternative to simply opening up the government's coffers to solve the digital divide is the option of creating new or revising existing federal laws, regulations, and tax policy.

An excellent example of revising federal law is how the Schools and Libraries Universal Service Fund (the "E-Rate") created by the Telecommunications Act of 1996 changed the fundamental notion of universal service. Under E-Rate, primary and secondary schools and libraries receive basic and advanced telecommunications services at discounts from 20 to 90 percent below commercially available rates.[41] The most disadvantaged schools and libraries (based on the percentage of students eligible for the national school lunch program), as well as those in rural areas, receive the highest discounts.[42] Financed with revenues from long-distance telephone charges, E-Rate provides approximately $2.25 billion in funds to schools and libraries.

Good examples of regulatory efforts are "open access" laws and regulations. To prevent monopolies on high-speed cable Internet access, open access regulations would allow the nation's nearly 8,000 Internet service providers to utilize the high-speed lines free of charge.[43] The basis for this lies in the fact that the telephone-based, dial-up Internet is required by law to be an "open" system.[44] This means telephone companies are prohibited from dictating how, or by whom, Internet service is provided.[45] However, without open access regulations, the cable company that owns the high-speed line can decide what news and information sources it wants to offer.[46]

Two prime examples of using tax policy to help solve the digital divide can be found in the Broadband Internet Services Act of 2000 and the Qualified Zone Academy Bond Program (QZAB). The Broadband Internet legislation calls for a five-year, two-tiered tax credit for companies deploying high-speed Internet access in disadvantaged areas.[47] Specifically, it gives a 10 percent tax credit for companies deploying 1.5-megabit service to rural and low-income areas, and a 20 percent tax credit for the deployment of 22-megabit service to rural and low-income customers.[48] Companies will not receive the tax credit until high-speed Internet access has penetrated a minimum of 10 percent of the targeted community.[49]

Congress, as part of the Taxpayers Relief Act of 1997, implemented the Qualified Zone Academy Bond Program (QZAB).[50] Starting in 1998, QZAB allocated $2.4 billion in tax credits over six years to the states on the basis of numbers of children in poverty. Private investors could purchase the tax credits and thus enable schools to borrow money interest free for the purposes of school rehabilitation and renovation. Schools serving Empowerment Zone and Enterprise Communities or those with student populations of 35 percent or more receiving free or reduced lunch could borrow money interest free to create a special academy that would enhance the skills and knowledge of the student population. To qualify for QZAB, the school needs to attract a business partner to place 10 percent of the bond's value in in-kind or cash contributions. National Education Foundation CyberLearning (www.cyberlearning.org) has provided the 10 percent contribution to school districts in many states.

QZAB uses the tax code to provide a way for the federal government to help underwrite the cost of technology and training while at the same time leveraging the resources of the private sector. Unlike traditional school bonds, the QZAB proceeds can be used to pay not just for equipment (computers), but also infrastructure repairs, like internal wiring. In addition, schools could be assured of long-term technical assistance and professional development services from a business partner.

Examples of State and Local Government Action

As shown before, many believe the digital divide is a pressing social and economic problem that requires immediate government action. Yet among those with this view, some feel that the federal government is too unwieldy, distracted, meddlesome, and/or inept to deal with the digital divide properly. Instead, they believe that government action on the digital divide must come from the state and local levels.

Several state governments are at the forefront in the action on the digital divide:

- A prime example is Maine's effort to provide every seventh-grader in the state with a free laptop computer that they would keep after graduation.[51] Using $50 million in state funds, along with $15 million from federal and private sources, each student in Maine will get a laptop on the first day of the seventh grade that, although the computers technically would be school property until graduation, students can take home for homework and research.[52] In addition, the plan would pay for the cost of equipping half of all the K–12 teachers in the state, with the local school districts paying for the other half.[53] Under the plan, 21,000 students and teachers would receive a free laptop in the first year of the program.[54]
- The North Carolina Information Highway (NCIH), an advanced broadband network linking state and public agencies, is being expanded to bring affordable, high-speed Internet access to all North Carolina citizens.[55]

- West Virginia's Senior Technology Initiative provides more than 200 computers to forty-four state-supported senior citizen centers.[56]
- Virginia has established two statewide programs at bridging the digital divide for its citizens. First is the Digital Opportunity Initiative established to "ensure that all Virginia citizens are able to participate in the benefits of a digital society."[57] Included in the initiative is the Virtual Opportunity Center, a clearinghouse of best practices and resource information available to community organizations, schools, and local governments.[58] Second is the Infopowering the Commonwealth program that aims at putting computers and high-speed Internet access in every Virginia library.[59]

On a local level, municipal governments are also taking the lead:

- The town of La Grange, Georgia, now pays for all of its citizens to receive Internet access via cable television, not personal computers.[60]
- In Atlanta, "cyber centers" have been set up by the city to provide computer training to children, adults, and senior citizens.[61] The cyber centers were established as part of an $8.1 million Community Technology Initiative funded by franchise fees paid by cable companies.[62]
- In Phoenix, residents have free Internet access through the city's six One Stop System sites and the thirty-two Electronic Community Access Model (ECAM) sites.[63]
- Boston is the perhaps the best example of local government action against the digital divide. Two notable programs within the city's Digital Bridge Boston initiative are TechBoston and Technology Goes Home. TechBoston is the citywide technology training program for public school students; in return for their high-tech training, students of TechBoston provide teachers, schools, and the Boston Public Library with IT support.[64] The Technology Goes Home program provides low-income families with a free computer, Internet access, and training.[65] Boston's Digital Bridge has produced some remarkable results:
  - In 1996 (the year before the program began), Boston had a student-to-computer ratio of 63 to 1, and only 5 to 10 percent of the city's public school teachers had access to a computer.[66]

○ In 2000, the student-to-computer ratio was 6 to 1, 65 percent of the public school teachers were trained in the effective use educational technology, and Boston had 130 networked schools, 100 networked community centers, and 26 networked libraries.[67]

OPTION 3: RELY ON PHILANTHROPY AND COMMUNITY ACTION

Outside of government action and free market solutions, many believe that the digital divide can be bridged through community efforts and philanthropy. The hope is that corporations, civic organizations, foundations, and individuals will realize the importance of the digital divide and act upon it like any other pressing public policy issue. The thought is that if America's long established volunteer and philanthropic spirit could be harnessed, the digital divide would quickly close.

One of the most vocal and eloquent voices in support of this option is the CEO of Hewlett-Packard, Carly Fiorina. In her view, society should look at the current gaps in technology access not as the "digital divide" but rather as an opportunity for "e-inclusion."[68] To Fiorina, to truly solve the problems of the digital divide, "we must give more than technology, more than just money."[69] Instead, the focus should be on nurturing voluntary acts of personal involvement in the problem, like "giving people career development paths, mentoring, [and] training."[70]

Examples of Philanthropy

Examples of individual and corporate philanthropy abound. The most publicized example of individual giving is Microsoft Chairman Bill Gates' donation of a whopping $1 billion to fund minority scholarships in technology fields.[71]

On a corporate level, philanthropy toward digital divide issues takes two forms. First, realizing the economic and social potential of a technology-empowered workforce, many private companies are giving free computers and discounted Internet access to their employees.[72]

For example:

- Ford Motor Company provides most of its employees with a computer, printer, and Internet access for $5.00 a month.
- American Airlines has given computers to 112,000 of its employees.
- Delta Airlines has given 72,000 of its employees computers.
- Intel Corporation has given 70,000 of its employees computers.

Second is the more traditional form of corporate philanthropy:

- The 3Com Corporation has donated $1 million in networking equipment and consulting services to ten U.S. cities to implement programs to help minorities and low-income families access the Internet.[73]

  - In Glasgow, Kentucky, for example, 3Com deployed a citywide network to link all residents to the public schools and city services.[74]
  - 3Com also installed computer kiosks throughout the city of New Orleans to reach students who have dropped out of school and those in danger of dropping out.[75] The purpose of the New Orleans computer network is to connect at-risk youth with training alternatives and job opportunities.[76]

- The computer maker Gateway offers $100 discounts off their PCs to anyone who donates a used, functional computer to Goodwill Industries.[77]
- The venture capital firm Flatiron Partners has given a $100,000 grant to provide incentives for providers of affordable housing to wire their units for computer hardware and Internet access.[78]

Many nonprofit foundations are also very active in closing the digital divide:

- One of the Verizon Foundation's primary funding areas is the digital divide. In addition, many of their other priority funding areas involve digital divide–related efforts: computer literacy, workforce development, and community technology development. Some of the Verizon's Foundation work includes:

  - Establishing an online resource center to assist schools and libraries to apply for the federal "E-Rate" program.
  - Offering $500,000 in workforce development grants to communities in Illinois and Indiana.[79]

- The eBay Foundation's Global Grants program support efforts to "increase technology skills and access." Some of the recent recipients include: [80]

  - The Para los Niños youth leadership program, which trains inner-city youths age eleven to eighteen to teach younger kids how to use computers.

- The Technology Training Foundation of America's Computers for Schools Program, which repairs donated computers and places them in public and private schools, after-school programs, student incentive programs, senior centers, battered women's shelters, and charitable organizations.
- Schools Online, an organization that donates Internet equipment to schools and facilitates teacher professional development and support.

- The Ford Foundation has supported several efforts to study and publicize the digital divide, like a report by the Consumer Federation of America and an outreach program organized by the Bay Area Video Coalition.[81]
- The National Education Foundation CyberLearning's main mission is bridging the digital divide. Hence, it offers matching grants for information technology/computer training to schools, colleges, and nonprofit organizations serving the disadvantaged in the United States and other countries: [82]

  - Provided a $3.7-million matching grant for IT training of teachers, students, and staff of the Yonkers (New York) Public School district.
  - Offers the Online IT Literacy Grant Program that provides 50 percent matching grants to disadvantaged schools, colleges, and community organizations, so that their teachers, students, and staff can enroll in online IT courses.
  - Offers the Online IT Professional Grant Program that provides 50 percent matching grants to schools, colleges, and community organizations, so that their teachers, students, and staff can receive advanced IT certification training.
  - Offers the Teacher Training Grant Program online as well as on site to all K–12 teachers serving the disadvantaged.

Examples of Community Action

As the digital divide brings with it a slew of society's ills (illiteracy, grossly uneven distribution of wealth, etc.), many diverse organizations are working in some part to close the digital divide. The following are a mere sampling of community-based organizations working directly against the digital divide:

- Community Action Resources and Development Inc. is an organization in Claremore, Oklahoma, that works with the local cooperative extension service, high school, and public library to provide free e-mail and Internet access to any resident of the county.[83]

- The Louisville and Jefferson County Community Action Agency of Louisville, Kentucky, offers computer training for low-income families.[84]
- The Multi-County Community Action against Poverty (Multi-CAP), based in Charlestown, West Virginia, remanufactures surplus computers from businesses, the government, and the state National Guard. MultiCAP has also established computer centers in HUD Assisted Housing Centers and Public Housing blocks.[85]
- Opportunities for Chenango offers free computer training for low-income seniors in the Norwich, New York, area.[86]
- Computers in Our Future operates eleven community technology centers in low-income areas throughout the state of California. The centers' goal is to "increase access to computer technology, teach marketable skills to area youth, and enhance job placement opportunities."[87]
- The Charles River Public Internet Center of Waltham, Massachusetts, works to "ensure that every member of the community has equal opportunity to become computer literate and has access to the Internet and office software."[88]
- The Columbia Technology Center provides Internet access, computer classes, and an open computer lab for rural Columbia County, Oregon.[89]
- Austin Free-Net provides free, public Internet access to all residents of Austin, Texas.[90]
- FairNet of Fairbanks, Alaska, is a community technology program that promotes computer/telecommunication literacy and Internet access to all people.[91]
- Chicago Cares offers the Partners in Technology Program (PITP) that "enables volunteers to bring technology to schools, community-based organizations, shelters, and nonprofits in some of Chicago's most under-resourced neighborhoods, giving adults and children access to computers, the Internet, and a brighter future."[92]

PRIVATE/PUBLIC PARTNERSHIPS

With the 2000 election came a shift in the federal government's priorities and attitudes towards the digital divide. The most immediate manifestation of this shift was the threat of the tap of government money being turned off and the deep pool of funding rapidly drying up. Around the same time, the high-flying, technology-fueled economy took a steep nose-dive. This meant many companies had to scale-back or abandon their sponsorship of and philanthropy to digital divide causes.

Therefore, the most practical solution is to form partnerships to share the burden running digital divide programs. Of the scores of partnerships formed to battle the digital divide, two stand out as the best examples.

Plugged In of East Palo Alto, California, offers free Internet access and computer training to the residents of one of poorest and most ethnically diverse areas of California. Beyond Internet and computer basics, Plugged In recruits a select number of students to participate in a ten-week training program that covers graphic design and HTML scripting. These training sessions are taught by volunteers from such companies as Intel, Sun Microsystems, and Cisco Systems. Through partnerships with some of Silicon Valley's biggest companies, Plugged In offers its students world-class, hands-on training in some of the most marketable Information Technology skills.[93]

PowerUp is unique because it is an amalgamation of nonprofits, businesses, and government agencies. Founded by America Online's Chief Executive Steve Case, PowerUp's main mission is to establish community-level computer and Internet centers throughout the nation. To accomplish this, PowerUp has received donations of 50,000 personal computers from the Waitt Family Foundation and 10,000 free Internet access accounts from AOL. The states of Illinois and Virginia (among others) have invested $750,000 and $3 million, respectively, to build PowerUp centers in their states.[94]

NOTES

1. Robert W. Crandall, "Universal Service, Equal Access, and the Digital Divide" (Washington, D.C.: Brookings Institution, December 2000).

2. Editorial, "Sorting Sense from Silly in Digital Divide," *The Seattle Times*, June 16, 2000.

3. Jube Shiver Jr., "Clinton Plan to Close 'Digital Divide' Called Unnecessary," *The Los Angeles Times*, January 29, 2000.

4. Jack Kemp, "Marketplace Will Bridge Digital Divide," *Copley News Service*, June 16, 2000.

5. Kemp, "Marketplace Will Bridge Digital Divide."

6. Adam B. Thierer, "Digital Divide or a Digital Deluge of Opportunity?" (Washington, D.C.: The Heritage Foundation, February 2000).

7. David Boaz "A Snapshot View of a Complex World," *IntellectualCapital.com* at www.intellectualcapital.com/issues/issue257/item5729.asp (accessed November 20, 2000).

8. W. Michael Cox and Richard Alm, *Myths of Rich and Poor* (New York: Basic Books, 1999).

9. Boaz "A Snapshot View of a Complex World."

10. Adam Clayton Powell III, "Is There Really a Digital Divide in America?" *The O'Reilly Network*, June 7, 2000.

11. Organization for Economic Co-operation and Development, "OECD Internet Access Price Comparison," September 21, 2000.

12. Adam D. Thierer, "How Free Computers Are Filling the Digital Divide" (Washington, D.C.: The Heritage Foundation, April 2000).

14. *Pricewatch.com* at www.pricewatch.com (accessed March 19, 2001).

15. *Pricewatch.com.*

16. *Pricewatch.com.*

17. *Pricewatch.com.*

18. Thierer, "How Free Computers Are Filling the Digital Divide."

19. *FreeDesktops.com* at www.FreeDesktops.com (accessed March 19, 2001).

20. *FreeDesktops.com.*

21. *FreeDiskSpace.com*, www.freediskspace.com (accessed March 19, 2001).

22. Thierer, "How Free Computers Are Filling the Digital Divide."

23. *FreeDiskSpace.com.*

24. *CyberTechHelp.com* at www.cybertechhelp.com (accessed March 19, 2001).

25. Gregory L. Rohde, Assistant Secretary of Commerce, "How Do We Know Where We Are Going if We Do Not Know Where We Are?" remarks to the European American Business Council, Washington, D.C., August 3, 2000.

26. Rohde, "How Do We Know Where We Are Going?"

27. "National Public Radio/Kaiser Family Foundation/Kennedy School of Government Survey of Americans on Technology," February 2000.

28. Don Tapscott, *Growing Up Digital* (New York: McGraw-Hill, 1997).

29. Tapscott, *Growing Up Digital.*

30. President's Information Technology Advisory Committee, "Using Information Technology to Transform the Way We Learn" (Washington, D.C.: GPO, February 2001).

31. U.S. Department of Labor Employment and Training Administration, at www.dol.eta.gov (accessed March 22, 2001).

32. U.S. Department of Education, at www.ed.gov/PressReleases/08-1999/wh-0824.html (accessed March 22, 2001).

33. Jill Rosen, "Bill Would Bring Computers to Thousands of Youths" at www.civic.com (accessed March 26, 2001).

34. Rosen, "Bill Would Bring Computers to Thousands of Youths."

35. Stephanie Ernst, "Bush, Gore Vow to Bridge Digital Divide" at www.DiversityInc.com (accessed March 16, 2001).

36. "How Do You Close the Digital Divide?" *Federal Computer Week,* September 18, 2000.

37. Patrick Ross, "New Congress Pitching Bevy of Broadband Bills," *CNET News*, March 5, 2001.

38. Technology for All Americans Act of 2000.

39. Technology for All Americans Act of 2000.

40. Technology for All Americans Act of 2000.

41. "Losing Ground Bit by Bit: Low-Income Communities in the Information Age," *The Benton Foundation* at digitaldividenetwork.org/content/sections/index.cfm?key=5 (accessed March 1, 2000).

42. "Losing Ground Bit by Bit," *The Benton Foundation.*

43. Paul Flatin, "Open Access on the Internet," www.policy.com, July 31, 2000.

44. Jeff Chester, "The Internet's Openness and Diversity Are at Risk," September 18, 2000, at www.tompaine.com.

45. Chester, "The Internet's Openness and Diversity Are at Risk."

46. Chester, "The Internet's Openness and Diversity Are at Risk."

47. Roy Mark, "Digital Divide Legislation Gains More Support," September 12, 2000, at www.internetnews.com.

48. Mark, "Digital Divide Legislation Gains More Support."

49. Mark, "Digital Divide Legislation Gains More Support."

50. U.S. Department of Education, at www.ed.gov/inits/construction/qzab.html (accessed March 21, 2001).

51. Jill Rosen, "Maine Proposes Laptops for Students," April 3, 2000, at www.civic.com.

52. Rosen, "Maine Proposes Laptops for Students."

53. Rosen, "Maine Proposes Laptops for Students."

54. Rosen, "Maine Proposes Laptops for Students."

55. The Southern Growth Policy Board, "Creating a CyberSouth," September 2000.

56. Eric Kulisch, "West Virginia Equipping Elderly with Computers," August 23, 2000, at www.civic.com.

57. Virginia Office of the Secretary of Technology, at www.sotech.state.va.us/digop.htm (accessed March 21, 2001).

58. Virginia Office of the Secretary of Technology, at www.sotech.state.va.us/digop.htm.

59. Iowa 2010 Commission, "Iowa's Digital Divide," at www.state.ia.us/government/its/Digital_Divide/Digital_Divide.htm (accessed March 21, 2001).

60. David Barry, "Internet Free for All in Georgia Town," *E-Commerce Times*, March 22, 2000.

61. Katie Dean, "Cyber Centers Burn Up Atlanta," *Wired News*, July 11, 2000.

62. Dean, "Cyber Centers Burn Up Atlanta."

63. National Association of Community Action Agencies, "Information Technology for Community Action Agencies and Their Low-Income Clients" (Washington, D.C.: Summer 2000).

64. Dan Page, "Building the Digital Bridge in Boston," *ConvergeMag* at www.convergemag.com/Publications/CNVGDec00/buildingDigital.shtm (accessed March 21, 2001).

65. Page, "Building the Digital Bridge in Boston."

66. Page, "Building the Digital Bridge in Boston."

67. Page, "Building the Digital Bridge in Boston."

68. Carly Fiorina, remarks before the Digital Connections Conference, San Jose, May 4, 2000.

69. Fiorina, remarks.

70. Fiorina, remarks.

71. Donna Ladd, "The Elitist Myth of Universal Access," *IntellectualCapital .com*, September 23, 1999.

72. Blake Bailey, "The Private Sector Is Closing the Digital Divide: Brief Analysis No. 331" (Washington, D.C.: National Center for Policy Analysis, August 2000).

73. Mary Hillebrand, "3Com Funds 'Digital Divide' Programs in 10 U.S. Cities," *E-Commerce Times*, January 31, 2000.

74. Hillebrand, "3Com Funds 'Digital Divide' Programs in 10 U.S. Cities."

75. Hillebrand, "3Com Funds 'Digital Divide' Programs in 10 U.S. Cities."

76. Hillebrand, "3Com Funds 'Digital Divide' Programs in 10 U.S. Cities."

77. "Gateway Offers PC Donation Incentive," *ResponsiblityInc.com* at www.responsibilityinc.com/Departments/DigitalDivide/gatewaygw.html (accessed March 21, 2001).

78. Silicon Alley News, "Flatiron Gives $100,000 to Bridge Digital Divide" at www.atnewyork.com/news/article/0,1471,8471_587481,00.html (accessed March 21, 2001).

79. The Verizon Foundation, at foundation.verizon.com/04001.html (accessed March 21, 2001).

80. The Ebay Foundation, at pages.ebay.com/community/aboutebay/ foundation/1998.html#2001 (accessed March 21, 2001).

81. The Ford Foundation, at www.fordfound.org/ (accessed March 21, 2001).

82. CyberLearning, at www.cyberlearning.org (accessed March 21, 2001).

83. National Association of Community Action Agencies, "Information Technology for Community Action Agencies and Their Low-Income Clients."

84. National Association of Community Action Agencies, "Information Technology."

85. National Association of Community Action Agencies, "Information Technology."

86. National Association of Community Action Agencies, "Information Technology."

87. *Computers in Our Future*, at www.ciof.org/ (accessed March 21, 2001).

88. *Charles River Public Internet Center*, at www.crpic.org/ (accessed March 21, 2001).

89. *Columbia Technology Center*, at www.columbia-center.org/home/ (accessed March 21, 2001).

90. *Austin Free-Net*, at www.austinfree.net (accessed March 21, 2001).

91. *FairNet*, at www.fairnet.org/ (accessed March 21, 2001).

92. *Chicago Cares*, at www.chicagocares.org/ (accessed March 21, 2001).

93. The Telecommunications and Information Infrastructure Assistance Program, "How Access Benefits Children: Connecting Kids to the World of Information," *U.S. Department of Commerce*, at www.ntia.doc.gov/otiahome/top/publicationmedia/How_ABC/How_ABC.html#part_five (accessed March 21, 2001).

94. Alec Klein, "Closing the Digital Divide," *The Washington Post*, at www.washingtonpost.com/ac2/wp-dyn?pagename=article&node=digest&contentId=A32559-2000 (accessed March 21, 2001).

CHAPTER 6

The Digital Divide Is a Digital Opportunity

Political will is the difference between a "digital divide" and a "digital opportunity" in development. Information technology, without the political will to use it to achieve development objectives, can increase the likelihood for an expanding digital "divide." The political will to use information and communication technology to achieve development objectives can be a digital "opportunity."

—Enrique V. Inglesias, president,
Inter American Development Bank[1]

Summary:

This chapter examines how today's "digital divide" challenge can be turned into tomorrow's opportunity. In order for many groups and populations to leapfrog ahead toward economic and social parity, they will need to advocate the digital divide issues within the political forum, develop strategic plans, and transform those plans into fundable proposals. This chapter offers guidance as to how to build an effective technology access and training program.

REVIEW OF THE DIGITAL DIVIDE

Because the digital divide combines social, economic, and cultural factors with public policy and technology issues, this book has had to touch upon a wide array of topics. By presenting all sides of the policy debate and focusing on the most recent surveys and reports, we have made every effort to be as objective and thorough as possible.

If there is any one conclusion to be drawn from the preceding chapters, it is the overwhelming importance of a comprehensive, strategic approach in dealing with both the causes of and solutions to the digital divide. Unequal access to technology is not merely a question of supply and demand. No matter how low computer prices and Internet fees drop, the pressing issues of effective IT training and quality education preparation still need to be addressed to ensure that all segments of the population can fully enjoy the benefits of the digital revolution.

In our view, the major benefit of the digital revolution is not the technology itself or its reinvention of commerce, governance, and societal interaction. Rather, the ultimate benefit of the digital revolution is the opportunity for disadvantaged and underserved groups to leapfrog ahead in a short time and gain parity with rest of society. In other words, the same digital revolution that caused the digital divide to separate society has also created a *digital opportunity* for economic and social equality. The only way to fully exploit this historic yet fleeting opportunity is to enable the disadvantaged and underserved with comprehensive IT access and training.

Chapter 1 showed that the digital divide still exists in the United States in 2002 because:

- Internet access is essential in today's society and economy, thus making it desirable to include Internet access in the ideal of a universal service.
- A large portion of the population is "unwired" due to *usability issues* (due both to the inherent complexity of technology and involuntary factors like disability and language abilities), *lack of education*, and *government barriers*.
- Beyond Internet access, the digital divide also encompasses access to broadband connections and usable content.
- The digital divide remains a major obstacle for low-income and rural communities, minorities, seniors, the disabled, and women.

Chapter 2 illustrated why the digital divide is an *urgent* problem by:

- Showing that the disadvantaged groups have a closing window of opportunity to gain social and economic parity, as illustrated by the parallels between the industrial and digital revolutions.
- Explaining how the technology haves and have-nots are growing apart and the risks this divergence presents.

- Demonstrating how the digital divide undermines the principles of American democracy and the threat it poses to the health of the economy.

Chapter 3 explored how the digital divide impacts education through:

- The lack of adequate technology training for teachers.
- The marked disparity in Internet-connectivity in high-poverty schools.
- The lingering shortcomings of the U.S. federal government's main program, the E-Rate.

Chapter 4 delineated the global digital divide by:

- Explaining the international digital divide between developed and developing nations.
- Cataloging the intraregional and intranational digital divides.
- Presenting the policies and programs of Australia, Canada, and Singapore as possible models for success.

Chapter 5 offered the four main policy options available to close the digital divide:

- Hope that the forces of a free market economy will eventually bring equal access and opportunity.
- Rely on government programs and funding.
- Trust in philanthropy and grassroots activism.
- Forge public/private partnerships to pool resources and expertise.

With this as a backdrop, the purpose of this chapter is to suggest that an *implementation strategy* for closing the digital divide, whether at the local neighborhood level or at a school district or state or national level, should be based on a thorough understanding of the issues discussed in the above chapters.

We strongly believe that if there is any one major conclusion to be drawn from what we have discussed in earlier chapters, it is that a comprehensive holistic strategic approach to understanding both the origins and the solutions to the digital divide is necessary. We need to understand that the issue of unequal access to technology is not merely a question of supply and demand. We need to include the issues of what types of educational preparation are necessary to use interactive technology effectively. This is not the same as training, which is also necessary but cannot substitute for a good experience in the use of information technologies to explore and advance understanding. In our view, society is confronted with a *digital opportunity*—a chance for disadvantaged groups to leapfrog ahead and gain parity.

WHAT IS DIGITAL OPPORTUNITY?

The blisteringly fast growth of information technology and its rapid rise to dominance in society and the economy has, without question, caused critical gaps in technology access. But it also presents a unique historic opportunity for visionary political, education, business, and community leaders to advance the lives of their constituents in a relatively short time period.

As outlined in chapter 2, when society moves from one age to the next, whether it be from the agrarian to the industrial, or from the industrial to the information as now, the disadvantaged or lagging segments of the society get a unique historic opportunity to leapfrog to equality in a short time, a few years, instead of going through the decades-long social-evolutionary process.

Today presents one of those rare, opportune times. We have a historic opening to transform the digital divide into the digital opportunity if we do the right things by providing our disadvantaged children and adults the opportunity to access and use information effectively.

Political and education leaders especially have a rare extraordinary chance to give their constituents parity by becoming visionary leaders bold enough to set goals, find the resources, and plan and implement student/adult-focused, outcome-based, integrated total solution programs such as our recommended CyberLearning or TTCM (Teacher/Training-Technology-Courseware/Content-Motivation) approach.[2]

A RECOMMENDED APPROACH: TTCM

It is a fact that many digital divide bridging programs fail because they are piecemeal rather than holistic in nature. In this post–September 11 climate of scarce resources, it is essential to provide a strategic solution to bridge the digital divide effectively. We favor a holistic cost-effective approach that addresses all the key elements necessary for a complete successful solution—Teacher/Training, Technology, Courseware/Content, and Motivation—and that provides multiple incentives to motivate people facing many stresses and discouraging life situations to improve their IT skills. We call it the TTCM approach.

- **T**, as in *Teacher/Training*: It is essential to provide students with skilled, committed teachers or mentors who are not only experts in their fields but also excellent communicators and motivators. While their title might be "trainer/teacher/mentor," since these people do so much mentoring and motivation, the title of "catalyst" might be more appropriate. Teacher training must be an essential component of any effective digital divide program.
- **T**, as in *Technology*: Three elements make up *Technology*: hardware (the most cost-effective and easy-to-use computer components), software (that facilitates the most relevant and valuable computer and Internet applications), and access (the opportunity to access information through Internet/CD, etc.).
- **C**, as in *Courseware/Content*: The lessons and content should be effective and results oriented, yet fun, engaging, dynamic, and interactive.
- **M**, as in *Motivation*: One of the most important yet often overlooked components of any learning program is motivation. For example, when we offered donated savings bonds or athletic shoes to inner-city disadvantaged students, their focus, motivation, enthusiasm, and effort levels all shot up significantly, especially when we offered them the opportunity to work on topics of interest to them, such as basketball.

Many digital divide programs fail because they focus on access to just computers and the Internet. A successful program should focus on using its limited resources effectively to train trainers/teachers/mentors, update technology to provide the right information to the right student at the right time, provide interesting and interactive courseware, and facilitate use of motivational tools, as the recommended TTCM approach attempts to do. Let us look at some considerations and examples related to Teacher/Training, Technology, Courseware/Content, and Motivation.

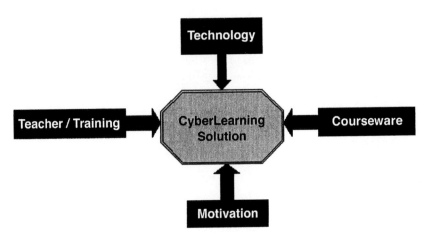

Figure 6.1. *Recommended solution.*

Teacher/Training

There is a consensus that training is a key to bridging the digital divide. Training considerations include access to training, the types of training, for whom and how that training is offered and how the training is paid for. There are three main areas to consider when developing training programs related to the digital divide:

Traditional K–12 education

To what extent are schools in the community capable of providing students with the skills they need?

A Typical Problem Addressed: Many schools located in high-poverty areas lack the resources both in terms of modern high-speed computers as well as qualified teachers to provide their students with the technology skills necessary.

A Successful Program Response: Cisco Systems, the leading world manufacturer of routers and switches, set up 6,000 plus "Networking Academies" that train more than 157,000 students located in twenty-six "Empowerment Zones" across all fifty states. The program offers training to students and teachers to design, build, and maintain computer networks.[3]

Workforce training

To what extent are those currently in jobs or are unemployed able to keep their skills upgraded so that they are employable in future jobs?

A Typical Problem Addressed: Very few minorities are entering IT professions. For example, in California, where Hispanic and African Americans constitute nearly 50 percent of the population, they make up only 7.9 percent of the IT professional employees in the Silicon Valley.

A Successful Program Response: The National Action Counsel for Minorities in Engineering (NACME) recruits minority talent by offering scholarships to minority students who select careers in engineering and specialized training programs in high school. NACME's Vanguard Program targets schools in poor, underserved communities and invites students to a series of workshops where problem-solving and nontraditional approaches to engineering are encouraged. Over the last decade, results have been impressive: over 20 percent of students who go through the program maintain a GPA of 3.5 or higher, and the program has a 98 percent persistence rate.

Community-wide training

To what extent are community residents, many of whom have dropped out or missed the technology revolution in some way, able to develop their own skills to participate in the new information economy?

A Typical Problem Addressed: The perception that it is hard to break into the IT field exists among many high-poverty community residents and prevents many from even starting to pursue IT fields, even on a part-time basis at a local community college.

A Successful Program Response: CitySkills.org has demonstrated that entry-level jobs in Web design are within the reach of underemployed urban adults. The program works because it offers Internet employers a pragmatic solution to the technology skills gap by offering screening, training, job referral, and placement. CitySkills.org has now expanded from the New York market to the national market. The program also helps those trying to create their own training programs in community technology centers, HUD community centers, and other local job training sites.

Technology

There is constant talk about the possibility that a technology breakthrough may diminish the needs for strenuous efforts to bridge the digital divide. If, for example, we could create a set-top box that would convert everyone's TV into a high performance, high-speed computer and the device could be sold cheaply, then perhaps we need not worry as much about access because TVs are so ubiquitous, at least among American households.

Another less utopian set of innovations concerns making the Internet more accessible to persons with disabilities. The computer and Internet revolution have not reached many people with disabilities. Only 25 percent of people with disabilities own a computer, compared with 66 percent of U.S. adults. And only 20 percent of people with disabilities have access to the Internet, compared to over 40 percent of U.S. adults.

The key obstacle to wider access is cost. Equipping computers with adaptive technology can cost as much as $20,000. Given the fact that the average income of Americans with disabilities is well below the national average, this is a huge barrier. Recently the U.S. federal government, through their publication of the Section 508 Regulation Requirements under the Americans with Disabilities Act, began requiring anyone who does business with the federal government to include those technical upgrades that will allow persons with the disabilities to benefit. For example, one provision of the new regulations requires alternative keyboard navigation, so that those who cannot operate a mouse or who have vision impairments can still navigate the Web. There are provisions that pertain to color and contrast settings, the use of animation, flash rate, and electronic forms, among others.[4] Technology exists to enable more people to benefit from the Web, but until the U.S. federal government makes it necessary for large corporations to invest in enabling voice translation, for example, of important Web-based documents for the blind, the likelihood is that market forces alone will not force companies to make the necessary investments.

For those who have faith in the market, it is likely that cutting-edge innovations, such as the new handheld devices, will provide, in the long term, cheaper and more convenient access to the Web. Just as laptops are replacing personal computers in many schools these days, we can look forward to a time when handheld devices will become as ubiquitous in schools as modern calculators. What will this mean for the digital divide? It is likely that the nature of the divide will shift. While millions of public school students may (through less expensive wireless technologies) be given a device that enables them to download full-motion video anywhere anytime, a greater premium will be placed on teachers' ability to fully extract the educational content using those new services. Thus, the game of "catch up" between advancing technologies and our ability to prepare people to take advantage of them will continue.

Paul Schroeder of the American Foundation for the Blind explains that closing the digital divide is about more than just providing affordable access. Millions of Americans will be left out unless more attention is paid to designing technology for the visually, hearing, and motor skill impaired. These disabled communities provide a viable market, according to Schroeder. Such technologies can also help those who are "situationally impaired." For example, a hands-free phone technology can help someone use the phone while driving a car; closed caption video can be used by those in noisy environments such as the airport, and wheelchair access ramps can assist those with baby strollers, dollies, and hand trucks. Moreover, Schroeder points out that Section 255 of the U.S. Telecommunications Act of 1996 requires that manufacturers of telecommunications equipment and providers of telecommunications services ensure that equipment and services are accessible to and usable by individuals with disabilities.

A central point that emerges is that there is no uniform definition for "access" as it pertains to the Internet. The accessibility issues have multiple dimensions that relate to such factors as income, race, gender, age, geography, and disability. There is discussion about the need to work on all aspects of access despite limited resources.

Now, about the appropriate role of government in the development of mechanisms for closing the digital divide, two viewpoints emerge. One view holds that there are profitable market opportunities to reach the segments of the community that are less connected to the Internet. The other position states that there will always be a market failure when it comes to reaching the poorest and least densely populated communities in America. These communities will require government support in order to get affordable Internet access.

Finally, there is general accord that the focus of government policy and private sector initiatives should be towards bringing access to American households, not just to community centers, schools, and libraries.

Courseware/Content

Part of the reason why the digital divide is such a powerful concept is that there exists an underlying assumption that the benefits of living in a digital age should accrue to all. In the minds of many, those benefits include, most significantly, an assumption that digitally based learning could provide a social and cultural breakthrough for millions of people locked out of traditional educational opportunities.

The belief in particular that Web-based education allows for "learning anytime and anywhere" has enabled e-learning companies to become one of the fastest growing sectors of the stock market. Corporate learning systems and for-profit universities have jumped in with both feet. In 1998, for example, $62.5 billion was spent on corporate training. Both publicly financed universities like the Western Governors University and for-profit universities such as the University of Phoenix have rushed into the e-learning market.

The omnipresent question in digital divide discussions is who is being left out and why? When it comes to e-learning, it is our contention that a lot more people are being left out than let in, almost inadvertently due to the problems of providing affordable high-quality content:

- Most computer-based training programs are nothing more than high-priced textbooks transferred to Web pages. In trying to appeal to every single audience and purpose imaginable, e-learning concerns have failed to properly target most learners' needs.
- Most content is in English and leaves out the growing Spanish-speaking populations in the United States and speakers of other languages around the world.
- Many courses are not interactive and so fail to engage the learners and help them assess their strengths and weaknesses.
- Most e-learning programs lack critical human support. Many people cannot learn just from interacting with a computer. People are needed (as we shall see in the next section) to help motivate, as well as to work with the problems that arise.

To get beyond these problems is a core challenge to digital-divide leaders. Although these problems have been solved by corporations that were determined to make e-learning profitable for their organizations, these solutions come with a price tag.

At CyberLearning, we believe we are a national digital divide leader in solving the problems related to poor or inappropriate content. We believe that successful e-learning programs that are targeted at the disadvantaged have to meet the following criteria:

- *High-quality course materials at a low cost.* There are a few e-learning vendors that have made the investments necessary to improve the quality of their offerings as judged by large numbers of users.

- *Available in languages other than English.* At the very minimum, they should support the growing American Spanish-speaking population.
- *Interactivity.* Courses should provide self-assessments and access to online teachers/mentors who can respond to questions either in real time or in a reasonable time period over the Internet.
- *Human support.* Learners struggling with difficult material, who have been out of school for a few years, or who have poor reading skills need all the help they can get. We strongly believe in the use of volunteers who can serve as coaches and mentors to disadvantaged students. Where this is impossible, we favor the use of phone and e-mail to reach distance learning mentors and coaches. One organization providing online mentors is the CompuMentor.org.
- *Coherent framework.* Instead of offering disconnected courses or units, we believe that to make a difference, high-quality content has to be related to clear goals and purposes. E-learners should be encouraged to see their learning within a larger scheme. For example, if a learner's aim is to become a network engineer or a programmer, it is rare that just taking one course will be sufficient. E-learners need to understand how a multiple number of course offerings relate to their goals. They should be given the self-assessment tools to identify which ones are appropriate. A common registration system and standardized reporting and monitoring system and an online schedule would advance this goal.

To bridge the digital divide, CyberLearning offers computer/IT scholarships for all disadvantaged school and college students, as well as disadvantaged schools, colleges, universities, and digital divide bridging organizations in the United States and other nations.

Motivation

Several basic commonsense ideas can quickly become lost in the excitement over the potential of e-learning. We know from our own experience with online programs in schools that students using computers and the Internet with a project-based curriculum demonstrate independent and critical thinking, and show improved abilities to find, organize, and evaluate information, and express their new knowledge and ideas in compelling ways. We also know that technology should always be seen as a means to an end and not the end itself. In other words, digital divide leaders should remember that they should build solutions that fit real needs, and that technology should be used as a useful tool.

It is much better to start with a small, manageable, well-defined project that meets a critical need than to build some large-scale "solution" that attempts too much and does not achieve concrete results. The key reason why small and focused solutions work better than those that are not is due in large part to the power of motivation. People need to feel that the problem they are trying to solve is important and that they can make a difference. Too often, digital divide planners omit this critically important element from their thinking, and, while the plans may "look good on paper," they fail a basic reality test.

An example of a successful program based on motivation is the Global Education Partnership (GEP). It relies on attracting youth with few alternatives into productive careers.[5] Headquartered in Oakland, California, the program provides high-poverty, disadvantaged students with the opportunity to start their own businesses using the tools of the digital age. For example, as relayed on the Benton Foundation's Digital Divide Network website, Ismael Cardenas grew up in a high-crime section of the San Francisco Bay area. He refused to join many of his peers in crime. Now, he runs his own Web development company thanks to skills he acquired from Global Education Partnership. In addition to the extra credits, he learned how to put a portfolio together, salesmanship, and earned a $500 scholarship grant that allowed him to start his Web company.

"GEP gave me the motivation to start my own business. My first idea was to start a T-shirt business because people like them in my neighborhood. Instead, I decided to build a website after attending the EETP," Ismael said.

As a Web designer, Ismael currently has five customers, and more are coming. Programs such as the GEP can be found in many parts of the United States and in many countries such as India, South Africa, Guatemala, and Indonesia.

Successful Community Technology Center programs recognize that it is important to begin with inner motivation and use technology as a tool to offer alternative ways for residents to reach their training and job goals than perhaps they were used to through traditional means:

- Brooklyn Public Library Literacy Program serves more than 850 adult beginning readers and writers. Students receive small-group instruction in basic literacy skills, including writing, reading, and computer and information technology.

- Old North End Community Technology Center (ONE CTC) is a nonprofit HUD-funded Enterprise Community program serving Chittenden County, Vermont. ONE CTC provides community-based training in basic computer skills to more than one hundred job seekers, unemployed persons, and residents each month. Computer courses help students to improve their skills on word processing, and business software applications.
- Plugged In, located in the heart of Silicon Valley, is a student-run business providing Internet-related services and Web-page design for clients from around the world. Through America Online, kids from Plugged In also facilitate a chat room for teenagers, discussing content such as affirmative action, gangs, drugs, and body piercing. Community members of all ages use state-of-the-art computers to do online research, work on resumes, complete homework assignments, or participate in one of thirty classes offered in partnership with local agencies. Serving more than 200 children and adults per week, Plugged In's community services include adult education, school-age education, open access, and computer classes.

TEN STEPS TO BRIDGING THE DIGITAL DIVIDE IN YOUR COMMUNITY

In order to successfully organize, plan, fund, implement, evaluate, and improve a project for bridging the digital divide in your community, you will find the following ten broad steps very useful:

1. *Needs Analysis.* The most important place to begin is to find out what local employers need from schools and community residents. Skill needs are constantly changing and digital divide grant writers need to design programs that take into consideration the fact that employers need not only just smart technical skills but also a number of soft skills. For example, today's workers need to know how to solve problems, as well as practice good work ethics. Appropriate attitudes towards customer service can sometimes be just as important as knowing how to write a spreadsheet program.

   Address real needs. As we know, top-down projects rarely work; you need to first assess what people want and are willing to use and/or pay for. In one project in India for example, male farmers said they needed information about agriculture; in fact, their largest single usage of the village info-kiosks was to get information about government programs.

2. *Define Objectives.* It is very important to define the objectives realistically. The objective statements should define the missions and visions clearly and concisely. For example, a poor rural community is not going to attract high tech jobs overnight, but it is possible to target a specific population that, if properly trained, could help move the entire community forward. A typical objective could be anything from helping all students in a high school to become IT-literate in a school year, to enabling some specific local businesses to take advantage of e-commerce.

The trouble with most vision statements is that they remain nice ideal propositions and do not have much staying power beyond the meeting where they were created. They need, in other words, to be implemented. To do this, they require a clear and specific focus, such as decreasing the number of dropouts through highly motivational after-school programs. The vision and mission may reflect a continuum of interconnected outcomes, for example, including (a) increasing test scores, (b) improved teacher training, and (c) reduction of unemployment rates.

3. *Gather Information.* Identify key stakeholders such as principals, teachers, students, parents, community leaders, business leaders, nonprofit leaders, religious leaders, government leaders, and others who have an interest in the project. Talk/communicate to them, note their levels of interest, and get suggestions.

Gather information on possible resources available, especially related to funds, space, teachers/mentors (volunteers and paid), technology (hardware, software, and Internet access), courseware, and motivation.

A link with an organization that can funnel resources into the community might be a good start. Prairienet (http://www.prairienet.org/) is one such example.[6] Prairienet is a member and donation-supported community network for Champaign-Urbana and the surrounding rural East-Central region of Illinois. Offered as a community service by the Graduate School of Library and Information Science at the University of Illinois at Urbana-Champaign, Prairienet's efforts are funded by donations, foundation grants, and a Telecommunications and Information Infrastructure Assistance Program.

Technical assistance from universities and colleges or private sector industries has to be a regular part of the effort. In order for a community to expand its efforts, it must be able to intelligently solve its technical questions. It must have people around who are smart enough to know what the technical questions are, and identify possible solutions. By involving local educational institutions, foundations, and private sector assistance, projects can have the long-term support they need to successfully implement the project and thus really make a difference.

4. *Build Coalitions.* Redefine your target population and goals based on feedback from the stakeholders. Prepare a one-page summary of the project and circulate it among the interested stakeholders. Create a project committee/team/board of interested and committed key decision makers among the stakeholders. Select a "doer" as the key committee person or director, who will organize the project cost effectively. Obtain initial funding from the stakeholders to carry out the planning.

Leadership: Sharing the power should be the goal of anyone who is interested in solving long-term problems connected with the digital divide. Necessary leadership skills include consensus building and willingness to share or rotate roles.

Involving community workers is also very important. Much of the work of community building is hard and uphill because most people in high-poverty community do not believe that their conditions can or will improve. They are skeptical of outsiders and cynical of change agents. Through hiring community organizers, some of that disbelief can start to change as they see their neighbors taking the issues seriously enough to attend meetings, hand out flyers, and generally rally their fellows. To do this effectively requires paying people for their time and trouble. Paid staff is the best route to go to maintain the quality of the effort.

5. *Define Goals.* Be specific. Choose goals that are action oriented, measurable, reliable, and timely. Specific measurable goals for a middle school digital divide project could be: number and percent of middle school students who pass tests indicating mastery of word processing, spreadsheet, database, and presentation; researching information on the Internet; or a basic knowledge of computer hardware and operating systems.

6. *Identify Resources.* Make a list of all the resources needed to accomplish the objectives. Specifically, identify the financial

resources, space, teachers/mentor qualifications and hours required, number and specifications of computers, software needed, Internet access (type and speed), course materials (online, CDs, books, etc.), and motivational resources needed to continuously motivate the participating students/adults to complete the program successfully. Identify additional resources needed by subtracting the available resources from the needed resources.

7. *Raise Funds.* There are many ways of raising funds, including community events, approaching wealthy individuals/organization for tax-deductible donations to an affiliated 501(c) (3) nonprofit (offer to name the program for them!), and, of course the most common way, writing grant proposals to foundations, corporations, government agencies, and other organizations. A website that will assist you with free guidance in writing proposals is Foundation Center (www.fdncenter.org). The site also helps you identify potential foundation funding sources.

8. *Develop an Implementation Plan.* Now, you are ready to develop a detailed implementation plan that will facilitate the orderly and cost-effective implementation of the project. This involves defining specific tasks and their milestones. Tasks are the specific activities that need to be performed. Milestones are the real benchmarks or indicators that help you gauge progress towards specific goals and objectives on a periodic basis.

First, list all the planning tasks and their milestones. Planning tasks include all the tasks that need to be completed before hiring of personnel and acquisition of equipment, space, and so forth. Planning tasks include making agreements; getting funding; developing pre- and post-tests; defining teacher/mentor qualifications; specifying mentoring methodology; developing curriculum; identifying selection criteria for acquisition of computers, software, Internet access, courseware, and motivational rewards; preparing and issuing requests for proposals (RFP); and similar tasks. For example, writing a grant proposal is a planning task. Securing a certain amount of funds by a certain date is a specific milestone.

Second, identify all the operations support tasks and their milestones. These are the tasks that need to be completed before the project operation begins. Such tasks include securing funds; preparing space; hiring mentors/teachers; training mentors/teachers; acquiring computers, software and Internet access; installing, integrating, and testing computers, software, and Internet access; acquiring course-ware, both online and hard copy such as books; and securing motivational rewards for the target students/adults.

Third, list all the operations tasks. These are tasks that will be conducted continuously during the project operation. Such tasks include providing mentored instruction/experience, transporting students, ensuring that the computers are fully functional and connected to the Internet, and providing snacks/motivational rewards to participating students/adults. For each task, list the milestones.

Fourth, list all the evaluation tasks, such as testing specific skills (such as word processing) and their milestones. The evaluation tasks and milestones should cover all the specific project goals/objectives. The evaluation of milestones on a periodic basis will allow the project team to make the necessary adjustments to continuously improve the program and to ensure that the program stays focused on meeting the objectives specified.

To control the cost, indicate in the implementation plan the projected cost of each task within each time period. This will allow you to monitor and control cost and budget by task on a weekly, monthly, or quarterly basis. A good implementation plan will enable you to view your project as a system. It will help you to plan, implement, evaluate, and improve on a continuous and dynamic basis.

In short, action planning is critical for any successful project. The plan should set out a timetable when specific changes (that is, new or modified programs, policies, and practices) will be implemented. The action plan should precisely state who is responsible for each action step/task and how that action step will be measured.

9. *Evaluate the Results.* This is a highly crucial step. Without regular record keeping and evaluation, the chances are slim that the project work will ever be replicated. Results have to be tallied and actions have to be taken promptly where objectives and performance fall short. Continuous data gathering and evaluation help to identify problems before they become crises. This management-by-systems, rather than the traditional management-by-crisis, approach will enable the project leaders to take corrective actions to solve the problems in a timely and cost-effective manner. Evaluation also determines the extent of success and ability to replicate of the project.

10. *Continue to Improve the Program.* Every program is dynamic. To keep up with the constantly changing needs and goals, project directors should keep using the evaluation data to continuously improve the program. Demonstration of success will also help to attract additional funds to improve and expand the program.

The ten steps listed above are dynamic and interactive. They need not be performed in the same order as above. Many times, you may go back and forth. For example, you may change your objectives to meet a specific requirement of a grant giver.

Some important points to remember are: stay focused; never lose sight of your vision, goals, and objectives; keep the stakeholders involved with a continuous stream of activities; and above all, make learning a fun experience for the participants.

For example, our CyberLearning approach employs a project method, that allows each participant team to choose a project topic of interest to team members, such as basketball or space. Then, the team members select a specific topic such as their favorite basketball player. Next, the team members go on the Web, explore, gather, and bookmark relevant information about their subject. This is followed by the mentor taking them through an online course on doing research on the Internet. We call this the learning-by-doing approach, meaning, do first and then take a related fun course.

The team then writes a one-page paper about the subject, followed by the mentor taking the team through a course on word processing. The team and the mentor repeat the same "do first and then take a fun course" steps for creating a database, spreadsheet, and graphic presentation on the subject.

Perhaps the most important facet of our approach is that it works for youngsters as well as adults. We have seen middle school students, with little or no exposure to computers, master the basic skills related to researching the Internet, word processing, spreadsheet, database, and presentation in a matter of a few hours when properly motivated.

How does a community not blessed with the types of resources that come from being situated in one of the nation's economic hubs begin to plan to ride the wave of the new digital economy and not just survive but thrive as it takes advantage of the new opportunities that the information revolution can bring? How do you know what solution is the right one for your community? How do you select from the range of solutions available?

Working with the community involves the building of partnerships. Partnerships cannot emerge out of thin air, however; they have to be stimulated by a common goal and purpose. The goal can rarely be more technology; it has to be defined in community terms—the need for better jobs, the need to improve the graduation and college attendance rates of students, the need to come up with safe and drug free schools. Most of the high-poverty communities we know suffer from the fact that their problems do not unite them; rather they split them into more and more fragments and sometimes competing agendas. Many are so overwhelmed with the multiple number of problems they face, the efforts of many volunteers and activists are focused on arresting the decline rather than working towards greater progress. The problem is often compounded by a lack of leadership, often preventing nonprofits and community-based organizations from sharing more of their resources and finding common goals.

While leaders who hope to solve the digital divide have to be able to avoid saying that technology will solve all your problems, they can say with some authority that, without technology, the solutions will come more slowly. At the center of any healthy community has to be the chance of good, quality jobs and a trained and educated workforce capable of competing for them. The problems of poor and underresourced schools, the tide of homelessness, AIDS and other health issues, drug abuse and alcohol addiction are symptoms, and not root causes of the problems these communities confront.

Because many of the higher paying and more skilled jobs today involve the use of technology (a Hudson Institute study found that, of the fifty-four careers with the highest job growth, only eight did not require computer skills), a powerful case can be made that the entire community has to realize that its future health and stability rests with the development of skills that enable more community residents to use the tools of the Information Age technology.

For example, in the area of grant writing, whether applying at the federal, state, or local level for resources to educate and train community residents, digital divide leaders need to be able to unify their residents around a clear vision. They need to link a clear vision statement with a concrete set of outcomes.

Remember, each one of us can make a difference by doing our part in bridging the digital divide. The satisfaction from making a difference, and thus making your community and this world a better place, is worth every effort!

Bridging the digital divide—both national and global—has assumed added significance since the events of September 11, 2001. We truly believe that the Internet and education provide increased opportunities, and consequently, lead to less terrorism. Let us hope that political, business, and community leaders everywhere can see the vision and act accordingly to convert the digital divide into a digital opportunity for their constituents, thus ushering their communities into the golden Information Age—a time for potential peace and prosperity for all!

NOTES

1. Enrique V. Inglesias, "From Digital Divide to Digital Opportunity in Latin America and the Caribbean," October 19, 2000.

2. *CyberLearning*, at www.cyberlearning.org.

3. "Cisco Networking Academy," *Cisco Systems, Inc.* at www.cisco.com/warp/public/779/edu/academy.

4. www.section508.gov/final_summary.html#technical.

5. *Digital Divide* at www.digitaldivide.org/guest_col.html.

6. *Prairienet Community Network* at www.prairienet.org.

7. *Digital Divide* at www.digitaldivide.org/guest_col.html.

Index

Note: Italicized page numbers refer to charts, tables, and figures.

About the Authors

Dr. Appu Kuttan is the founder and chairman of National Education Foundation CyberLearning, a national and global leader in bridging the digital divide. Dr. Kuttan is also a noted management and education systems innovator and the author of many innovative concepts and books, including "CyberLearning" (Teacher/Training-Technology-Courseware/Content-Motivation), "Management By Systems" (Goals-Objectives-Resources), "Total Tennis" (Mental Toughness-Conditioning-Strategy-Weapon Strokes), and "Holistic Executive" (Mind-Body-Soul).

Applying these concepts, Dr. Kuttan has helped to improve Venezuela's social security and health care system, India's national plan implementation program, Puerto Rico's traffic safety, the University of Puerto Rico's MBA and industrial engineering programs, U.S. Tennis, and information technology training in the United States and other countries. As chairman and major shareholder of the famous Nick Bellettieri Tennis Academy, Dr. Kuttan helped to develop many world tennis champions, including Andre Agassi, Monica Seles, and Jim Courier. Dr. Kuttan has advised many world leaders, including Rajiv Gandhi, and has been a mentor to many young celebrities, including tennis star Monica Seles and U.S. Presidential Honoree and Stanford JD-MBA standout Roger Kuttan.

Dr. Laurence Peters is the director of the Mid-Atlantic Center on Technology in Education Consortium at Temple University and a vice president of National Education Foundation CyberLearning.

Previously, Dr. Peters held senior positions at the U.S. Department of Education and specialized in helping to bridge the digital divide. He helped conceptualize U.S. administrative policy concerning strategies to enable high-poverty schools, particularly those located in Empowerment Zones and Enterprise Communities, and to bridge the digital divide through the delivery of government surplus computers, teacher training, and partnerships with technology companies. He has authored many articles on issues related to educational technology.